GRAMMAR WORKBOOK

EXERCISES
in ENGLISH

LEVEL
D

LOYOLAPRESS.

CHICAGO

Consultants

Therese Elizabeth Bauer
Martina Anne Erdlen
Anita Patrick Gallagher
Patricia Healey
Irene Kervick
Susan Platt

Linguistics Advisor

Timothy G. Collins
National-Louis University

Series Design: Loyola Press
Interior Art:
Jim Mitchell: 5, 15, 22, 36, 46, 56, 88, 98, 101.
Greg Phillips: 25, 26, 30, 58, 75, 86.
All interior illustrations not listed above are by Heather Kezdy.

ISBN-10: 0-8294-2336-2; ISBN-13: 978-0-8294-2336-5

Exercises in English® is a registered trademark of Loyola Press.

Manufactured in the United States of America.

06 07 08 09 10 11 12 VonH 10 9 8 7 6 5 4 3 2 1

Contents

iv

DIAGRAMMING

Name _____

1. Sentences—Part I

A **sentence** is a group of words that expresses a complete thought. Every sentence begins with a capital letter. A sentence has a subject and a predicate. The subject is who or what the sentence is about. The predicate tells about the subject.

SUBJECT	PREDICATE
Most rain forests	**grow in the tropics.**

A. Read each example. Write **S** if the group of words is a sentence. Put a period at the end of each sentence.

_____ 1. Most rain forests are hot and humid

_____ 2. Many kinds of plants and animals live in rain forests

_____ 3. Hundreds of different kinds of birds

_____ 4. The birds eat seeds, fruit, and insects

_____ 5. Nests in the tall trees

B. Make statements by matching the words in the first column with the words in the second column. Write the correct letter on the line. Use each letter once.

1. The sun shines _____

2. Plants use _____

3. The food in plants _____

4. There is solar energy _____

5. Animals eat plants _____

a. contains solar energy.

b. to get energy.

c. every day on the rain forest.

d. sunshine to make food.

e. in leaves, stems, and roots.

6. An insect _____

7. A bird can get energy _____

8. Some snakes eat _____

9. All animals get _____

10. Plants and animals _____

f. by eating insects.

g. eats a leaf and gets energy.

h. are all part of the food chain.

i. energy from food.

j. birds to get energy.

2. Sentences—Part II

A **declarative sentence** makes a statement. It ends with a period.

Gold is a valuable metal.

An **interrogative sentence** asks a question. It begins with a question word or with a verb. It ends with a question mark.

Do you know how gold is mined?

A. Decide whether each sentence is declarative or interrogative. Write your answer on the line.

_____ 1. What happened on January 24, 1848?

_____ 2. Gold was found at the edge of a river in California.

_____ 3. By May the streets of San Francisco were almost empty.

_____ 4. Where had everyone gone?

_____ 5. Almost everyone had headed for the gold fields.

_____ 6. In 1849 about 90,000 Americans journeyed to California.

_____ 7. Were they called forty-niners?

_____ 8. The discovery of gold changed California's history.

_____ 9. People came from all over the world to find riches.

_____ 10. How many do you think were disappointed?

B. Decide whether each sentence is declarative or interrogative. Write your answer on the line. Add the correct end punctuation.

_____ 1. Where is gold usually found

_____ 2. Gold can be found in veins in rocks

_____ 3. Sometimes gold is found in rivers or creeks

_____ 4. Why is gold so expensive

_____ 5. Gold is a very rare metal

3. Question Words

A question can begin with *who, what, when, where, why,* or *how.*

Potatoes are an important crop in Idaho.
What are an important crop in Idaho?
Where are potatoes an important crop?

Rewrite each declarative sentence as a question.
Use the question word given.

1. Tubers are part of the underground stem system of a potato plant.
   What _____?

2. Potato plants store food in the tubers.
   Where _____?

3. The tuber is the edible part of the potato plant.
   What _____?

4. Ancient people of Peru developed a technique to freeze-dry potatoes.
   Who _____?

5. Europeans first saw potatoes in the 1500s in South America.
   When _____?

6. Spanish conquistadors took potatoes from South America to Europe.
   Who _____?

7. Later, European settlers brought potatoes to North America.
   Who _____?

8. Thomas Jefferson served French fries in the White House.
   What _____?

9. Today the potato is the world's fourth-most-important food crop.
   What _____?

10. Potatoes are grown in some 130 countries around the world.
    Where _____?

4. Sentences—Part III

> An **imperative sentence** gives a command or makes a request. It usually ends with a period.
>
> **Try to eat a healthful diet.**
>
> An **exclamatory sentence** expresses strong emotion. It ends with an exclamation point.
>
> **Stir-fried food is delicious!**

A. Decide whether each sentence is imperative or exclamatory. Write your answer on the line. Add the correct end punctuation.

1. _____ Chop meat and vegetables into bite-sized pieces

2. _____ Heat a small amount of oil in a skillet

3. _____ Stir in the meat and vegetables

4. _____ Be careful

5. _____ Don't burn yourself

B. Rewrite each sentence as a command.

1. You can bake a potato with the rays of the sun on a very hot day.

_____

2. You have to get a potato and a small basket lined with aluminum foil.

_____

3. You should push a clean nail through the bottom of the basket.

_____

4. You have to stick the potato on the nail.

_____

5. You should turn the cooker to face the sun as it moves across the sky.

_____

Name _____

5. Four Kinds of Sentences

A sentence can be declarative, interrogative, imperative, or exclamatory.

Put the correct punctuation mark at the end of each sentence.

1. Ida B. Wells was a schoolteacher in Tennessee

2. On May 4, 1884, she got on a train to go to work

3. The conductor told her to move out of the first-class coach

4. He said black people had to ride in the smoking car

5. Miss Wells was absolutely furious

6. What could she do to help other black people

7. She decided to become a newspaper reporter

8. In 1892 some friends of hers were lynched by a mob

9. How horrible that was

10. Ida wrote articles against lynching

11. She made speeches all over the United States and in England

12. Did her work have any effect

13. The federal government took action to protect black people

14. Ida also worked for the suffrage movement

15. She wanted all citizens to be able to vote

 Ida B. Wells worked tirelessly for equal justice for all. Give an example of how you can help to see that everyone is treated fairly.

6. Subjects and Predicates

Every sentence has a subject and a predicate. The **complete subject** includes the name of the person, place, or thing the sentence is about and all the words that go with it. The **complete predicate** includes the verb and all the words relating to it. It describes what the subject is or does.

COMPLETE SUBJECT   COMPLETE PREDICATE

The Pony Express   was a mail service between Missouri and California.

A. Draw a vertical line between the complete subject and the complete predicate of each sentence.

1. More than 180 men rode for the Pony Express.

2. The Pony Express route was almost 2,000 miles long.

3. Each Pony Express rider covered 75 to 100 miles.

4. A fresh horse was provided every 10 to 15 miles.

5. The original cost of mailing a letter was $5.00 per one-half ounce.

B. Underline the complete subject of each sentence once. Underline the complete predicate twice.

1. A riderless horse galloped into the Pony Express station in Sacramento.

2. Its rider had been killed by Indians.

3. Eleven-year-old Broncho Charlie Miller caught the horse.

4. The boy jumped on the horse.

5. He carried the mail to Placerville.

6. Broncho Charlie was the youngest Pony Express rider.

7. Buffalo Bill put Charlie in his Wild West Show.

8. Charlie rode from New York to San Francisco many years later.

9. The ride commemorated the 70th anniversary of the Pony Express.

10. Broncho Charlie Miller lived to be 105 years old.

7. Simple Subjects

Every sentence has two important parts. These parts are called the subject and the predicate. The **subject** names the person, place, or thing talked about in the sentence. The most important word in the subject is usually a noun. This noun is the **simple subject**. To find the subject, ask the question *who* or *what* before the predicate.

COMPLETE SUBJECT
The cool, fresh air is made up of matter.
(*What* is made up of matter?)

SIMPLE SUBJECT
This matter is a mixture of gases.
(*What* is a mixture of gases?)

Underline the simple subject in each sentence.

1. Air is tasteless and odorless.

2. Our precious air is also invisible.

3. Gases make up air.

4. All gases take up space and have weight.

5. Gases are made up of tiny particles.

6. These tiny particles are called molecules.

7. The molecules are moving constantly.

8. Nitrogen makes up most of the air, about 78 percent.

9. Oxygen makes up about 21 percent of the air.

10. Other gases make up 1 percent of the air.

11. Earthly life is possible because of these gases.

12. Plants use carbon dioxide and sunlight to make food.

13. This process is called photosynthesis.

14. Oxygen is produced during photosynthesis.

15. All people need oxygen to breathe.

8. Simple Predicates

> The predicate of a sentence describes what the subject does or is. The predicate always contains a verb. The verb is the **simple predicate**.
>
> COMPLETE PREDICATE
> **Explorers <u>travel</u> to other lands.**
>
> SIMPLE PREDICATE
> **They often <u>write</u> about their adventures.**

Underline the simple predicate in each sentence.

1. Marco Polo lived in Venice, Italy, about 700 years ago.

2. He wanted a life of adventure.

3. In 1271 he, with his father and his uncle, started an overland journey to China.

4. After many new and strange experiences, they reached China in 1275.

5. The ruler, Kublai Khan, welcomed the Polos to his kingdom.

6. Kublai Khan appointed Marco to high positions in the government.

7. In China, Marco saw paper money for the first time.

8. The Polos stayed in Kublai Khan's court for 17 years.

9. They returned to Venice in 1295 with a treasure of gold and jewels.

10. Later Marco captained a ship against one of Venice's enemies.

11. The foes captured Marco during the battle.

12. While a prisoner, he wrote an account of his travels and adventures.

13. The book immediately became a bestseller.

14. It paved the way for thousands of travelers after him.

15. Marco Polo died a rich man in 1324.

9. Compound Subjects

> A **compound subject** has two or more simple subjects.
> The subjects are joined by *and* or *or*.
>
> SIMPLE SUBJECT
> **A <u>moose</u> eats twigs and leaves.**
>
> COMPOUND SIMPLE SUBJECT
> **<u>Moose</u> and <u>deer</u> eat twigs and leaves.**

A. Underline each noun in the subject.

1. Biologists and zoologists observe animal life.
2. Walruses, whales, and sea lions are large mammals.
3. Seals, reindeer, and elephants live in family groups called herds.
4. Sharks and piranhas attack with their sharp teeth.
5. Female wallabies and koalas keep their young in pouches.
6. Gophers and badgers live in burrows under the ground.
7. Snails and clams are both classified as mollusks.
8. Frogs, toads, and salamanders live in wet environments.
9. Oysters and mussels have protective hard shells.
10. Penguins and polar bears have adapted to very cold climates.

B. Combine each group of sentences into one sentence with a compound simple subject. Add correct end punctuation.

1. Dodos are now extinct. Auks are now extinct.

_____

2. Dogs can dream. Cats can dream.

_____

3. Spiders are not insects. Centipedes are not insects.

_____

4. Hamsters are often kept as pets. Gerbils are often kept as pets.

_____

5. Horses have hooves. Donkeys have hooves. Mules have hooves.

_____

Name _____

10. Compound Predicates

> A **compound predicate** has two or more simple predicates.
> They are joined by *and, but,* or *or.*
>
> SIMPLE PREDICATE
> **A teacher <u>instructs</u> students.**
>
> COMPOUND SIMPLE PREDICATE
> **A seamstress <u>cuts</u> and <u>sews</u> cloth.**

A. Underline the compound simple predicate twice in each sentence.

1. A gardener weeds and waters plants.

2. A nurse cleans and bandages wounds.

3. A scientist conducts and reports experiments.

4. A rodeo cowboy rides and ropes animals.

5. An administrative assistant answers the phone, sends faxes, or types letters.

B. Write complete sentences with compound simple predicates.

1. An artist _____

_____

2. A farmer _____

_____

3. A basketball player _____

_____

4. A student _____

_____

5. I _____

_____

11. Direct Objects

The **direct object** is the noun or pronoun that completes the action of the verb. Many sentences need a direct object to complete their meaning. To find the direct object of a sentence, ask *whom* or *what* after the verb. A sentence with more than one direct object has a compound **direct object**. The direct objects are connected with *and* or *or.*

DIRECT OBJECT
The first cars scared many people.   (Cars scared *whom?*)

COMPOUND DIRECT OBJECT
Travelers once used horses and buggies.   (Travelers used *what?*)

A. Circle the direct object in each sentence.

1. The first cars worried townspeople.
2. Some towns soon passed speed-limit laws.
3. Cars could not exceed those limits.
4. Towns did not have street signs or stoplights.
5. Officials installed signs right away.
6. Henry Ford loved the idea of cars.
7. Happily he watched other people in cars.
8. One day people would buy cars.
9. Henry opened a factory to build cars.
10. He started the Ford Motor Company in 1903.

B. Complete each sentence with a direct object from the list. Use each term once.

| car | method | Model T cars | step | time |

1. In Ford's factory, workers built _____.

2. One worker did not build an entire _____.

3. Instead, each person on the assembly line completed just one _____ in the process.

4. One worker's repetition of the same job saved _____ and money.

5. Now most factories use the assembly-line _____.

12. Subject Complements

A **subject complement** is usually a noun or an adjective that tells more about the subject. It follows a linking verb, such as the verb *be* and its various forms *(am, are, is, was, were)*. Two simple subject complements joined by *and, but,* or *or* form a **compound subject complement**.

SUBJECT	LINKING VERB	SUBJECT COMPLEMENT	
Rain forests	**are**	**home**	**to many animals.**
A rain forest	**is**	**humid**	**all year.**

Underline the simple or compound subject complement in each sentence.

1. The red-eyed tree frog is a very colorful animal.

2. The frog's most startling characteristic is its huge red eyes.

3. Its body is mostly green.

4. Some parts of the body are blue and yellow.

5. The frog's upper legs are usually bright blue.

6. Its feet are bright orange or red.

7. They are important for the animal's survival.

8. Suction-cup toe pads are useful for climbing trees.

9. The red-eyed tree frog is a carnivore.

10. Leaf frog is another name for this rain-forest animal.

13. Compound Sentences

> Two short sentences that are related to each other can be combined into a **compound sentence.** To combine the sentences, add a comma followed by *and, but,* or *or.* The first word in the second part of the compound does not start with a capital letter unless it is *I* or the name of a person or place.
>
> TWO RELATED SENTENCES
> **Sharks are fish.**
> **Whales are mammals.**
>
> COMPOUND SENTENCE
> **Sharks are fish,**
> **but whales are mammals.**

A. Write *and, but,* or *or* to complete each compound sentence.

1. A shark's skeleton is made of cartilage, _____ it has no real bones.

2. Most fish can swim backward, _____ sharks can only swim forward.

3. Sharks can be a few inches long, _____ they can be as big as a bus.

4. Great white sharks are rare, _____ they are being protected.

5. Sharks existed before the dinosaurs, _____ they are found all over the world.

B. Combine each pair of sentences into a compound sentence. Use a comma and *and, but,* or *or.*

1. Sharks may have 3,000 teeth. They do not usually chew their food.

   _____

2. Some sharks are fast swimmers. These sharks are fierce predators.

   _____

3. Sharks do not sleep as we do. They have active and inactive periods.

   _____

4. Sharks are intelligent. They can learn as quickly as rats and birds.

   _____

5. Almost all sharks are carnivores. They do not usually attack people.

   _____

14. Run-on Sentences

A **run-on sentence** results when two sentences are combined but not connected properly. The related sentences are separated by only a comma or by no connectors at all. To fix a run-on sentence, you can make a compound sentence with a comma and *and, but,* or *or.* If the sentence is very long, you can make two shorter sentences.

RUN-ON SENTENCE	**Redwoods grow in California, they are the tallest living trees.**
CORRECTION	**Redwoods grow in California, and they are the tallest living trees.**
RUN-ON SENTENCE	**Many redwoods are 600 years old some have lived 2,000 years.**
CORRECTION	**Many redwoods are 600 years old, but some have lived 2,000 years.**

Rewrite these run-on sentences as compound sentences.

1. Bristlecone pines grow in the West, they are some of the earth's oldest living things.

   _____

2. These trees live in six western states the oldest ones are in Colorado.

   _____

3. Spring arrives there in May, there are only three warm summer months.

   _____

4. The wind blows all the time some years only 10 inches of rain fall.

   _____

5. Few trees can live in these windswept places, bristlecone pines have adapted.

   _____

Name _____

15. Reviewing Sentences

A. Underline the simple subject in each sentence.

1. Elizabeth Blackwell was born in 1821 in Bristol, England.

2. Elizabeth had four sisters and four brothers.

3. At that time most girls did not receive good educations.

4. Elizabeth's father hired fine private tutors for her and her sisters.

5. Elizabeth's education would help her in the future.

B. Underline the simple predicate in each sentence twice.

6. In Elizabeth's 11th year the family moved to the United States.

7. After her father's death the family needed money.

8. Elizabeth and her sisters gave music and English lessons to local children.

9. Elizabeth helped many people.

10. One day Elizabeth visited a sick woman.

C. Circle the direct object in each sentence.

11. Elizabeth's sick friend had a secret.

12. Her male doctors didn't understand women well.

13. She presented an idea to Elizabeth.

14. Elizabeth would pursue a career in medicine.

15. Sixteen medical schools denied Elizabeth admission.

CONTINUED

D. Underline the compound simple predicate in each sentence twice.

16. Finally she successfully argued and won her case for admission.

17. A college in New York explained the situation and asked its students to vote on admission for Elizabeth.

18. Probably as a joke, the all-male student body voted and accepted her.

19. Elizabeth studied hard and graduated from medical school.

20. She imagined and then founded the first women's medical college.

Elizabeth Blackwell fought for fair treatment of women. Give an example of something you can do to help society be fair to women.

Try It Yourself

Write four sentences about helping with a chore around the house. Include direct objects, at least one compound simple subject, and at least one compound simple predicate.

_____

_____

_____

_____

Check Your Own Work

Choose a piece of writing from your portfolio, a work in progress, an assignment from another class, or a letter. Revise it, using the skills you have reviewed. This checklist will help you.

✔ Do your sentences express complete thoughts?

✔ Have you used direct objects correctly?

✔ Were you able to use compound subjects or predicates in your sentences?

Name _____

16. Nouns

> A **noun** names a person, a place, or a thing.
> **Animals use different parts of their bodies for different needs.**

A. Underline the nouns in each sentence.

1. African elephants use their big ears to help them cool down.

2. Blood passes through their ears and sends heat out into the air.

3. Hungry elephants can use their tusks to break apart trees to get to the soft pulp inside.

4. Thirsty elephants use their tusks to dig for water in dry ground.

5. After they find water, elephants suck it up with their trunks and put it in their mouths.

6. Polar bears live in regions covered by snow and ice.

7. These bears have thick fur that keeps them warm.

8. The fur of a polar bear is colorless, not white.

9. Sunlight passes through the clear fur down to the bear's skin.

10. The bear's skin is dark and takes in the heat from the sun.

B. Complete each sentence with a noun or nouns.
Use each word once.

bat	homes	blood	poison	eggs
ground	spaces	holes	teeth	

1. Many animals use their _____ in interesting ways.

2. A vampire _____ uses its sharp teeth to drink _____.

3. Some snakes shoot _____ through hollow _____ in their teeth (fangs) to kill other animals.

4. Other snakes make _____ in _____ to suck out the yolks.

5. Gophers use their big front teeth to help dig _____ in the _____.

17. Common Nouns and Proper Nouns

> A **common noun** names any one member of a group of persons, places, or things. A **proper noun** names a particular person, place, or thing. It begins with a capital letter.
>
> COMMON NOUNS
> The United States has many <u>climates</u> and <u>habitats</u>.
> A <u>state</u>, such as California, can have <u>mountains</u> and <u>deserts</u>.
>
> PROPER NOUNS
> The <u>United States</u> has many climates and habitats.
> A state, such as <u>California</u>, can have mountains and deserts.

A. Circle each common noun. Underline each proper noun.

1. The United States has different regions
   with many kinds of weather.
2. What is the climate like where you live?
3. Polar bears live in the cold climate of Alaska.
4. The flat plains of Kansas are used to grow wheat.
5. In a desert it is very hot and dry during the day.
6. The Mojave Desert is in parts of California and Arizona.
7. Large amounts of rain fall in the state of Washington.
8. The state of Minnesota has many lakes.
9. Florida is home to the Everglades, a warm and wet swamp.
10. The Rocky Mountains are famous for their beauty in winter.

B. Match a proper noun from the first column with the related common noun from the second column. Write the correct letter on the line.

_____ 1. Pacific   a. building

_____ 2. George Washington   b. amusement park

_____ 3. Utah   c. president

_____ 4. White House   d. state

_____ 5. Disney World   e. ocean

Name _____

18. Singular Nouns and Plural Nouns

A **singular noun** names one person, place, or thing. A **plural noun** names more than one person, place, or thing. The plural of most nouns is formed by adding -s to the singular. The plural of nouns ending in s, x, z, ch, or sh is formed by adding -es to the singular.

SINGULAR	PLURAL	SINGULAR	PLURAL
bag	**bags**	**box**	**boxes**

The plural of a noun ending in y after a consonant is formed by changing the y to i and adding -es. The plural of a noun ending in y after a vowel is formed by adding -s.

SINGULAR	PLURAL	SINGULAR	PLURAL
baby	**babies**	**boy**	**boys**

Nouns

A. Write **S** if the noun is singular or **P** if it is plural.

1. peaches _____

2. grape _____

3. berries _____

4. plums _____

5. banana _____

6. onion _____

7. peppers _____

8. tomatoes _____

9. carrot _____

10. beans _____

B. Write the plural for each of these singular nouns.

1. seal _____

2. daisy _____

3. ferry _____

4. fox _____

5. kite _____

6. bench _____

7. jury _____

8. paint _____

9. play _____

10. dish _____

19. More Singular Nouns and Plural Nouns

A. Circle each singular noun. Underline each plural noun.

1. Never play with matches.

2. Do not lean out of an open window.

3. Lock up all medicines in a safe place.

4. Turn out all lights before leaving the house.

5. Do not put metal in the microwave.

6. Do not leave a room where water is running.

7. Lock the cabinet or closet where detergents are kept.

8. Do not open the door to strangers.

9. Keep perishable foods in the refrigerator.

10. Know where to find a flashlight.

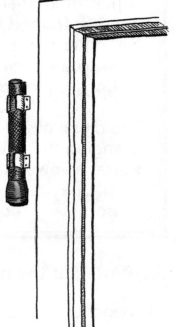

B. Complete each sentence with the plural of the noun at the left.

stair   1. Walk, do not run, on the _____.

compass   2. Be careful with sharp objects such as _____ and scissors.

door   3. Close classroom _____ quietly and slowly.

instruction   4. When there is a fire drill, follow your teacher's _____.

classmate   5. Be polite and respectful to your _____.

tool   6. Keep _____ in good order and in their proper places.

sport   7. When you play _____, follow the rules.

stranger   8. Report any _____ in the hallways to a teacher.

problem   9. Solve _____ with a classmate rather than argue.

class   10. Get to your _____ on time.

20. Irregular Plural Nouns

The plurals of some nouns are not formed by adding *-s* or *-es* to the singular. These are called **irregular plurals.** Some nouns change spelling to make the plural. Other nouns have the same form in the singular as in the plural. Irregular plurals must be memorized. If you cannot remember how to spell an irregular plural, look in a dictionary.

SINGULAR	PLURAL		SINGULAR	PLURAL
child	children		tooth	teeth
knife	knives		foot	feet
sheep	sheep		series	series

A. Write the plural for each of these singular nouns.

1. man _____   6. salmon _____

2. goose _____   7. mouse _____

3. woman _____   8. wolf _____

4. deer _____   9. ox _____

5. tooth _____   10. child _____

B. Complete each sentence with the correct form of the noun in parentheses. Write **S** if the form is singular or **P** if the form is plural.

_____ 1. The three _____ had a great time at the farm. (child)

_____ 2. They saw a _____ honking in the yard. (goose)

_____ 3. A pair of _____ was pulling a wagon. (ox)

_____ 4. A young _____ was working in a garden. (woman)

_____ 5. Several _____ were picking apples. (man)

_____ 6. Three _____ were grazing in a meadow. (sheep)

_____ 7. Several field _____ ran from the barn. (mouse)

_____ 8. A _____ was running through the woods. (deer)

_____ 9. A big _____ jumped in the pond. (catfish)

_____ 10. The children dipped their _____ in the pond. (foot)

21. Singular Possessive Nouns

Nouns

> A **possessive noun** shows possession or ownership. A singular possessive shows that one person or thing owns something. It is formed by adding an apostrophe (') and the letter *s* ('s) to a singular noun.
>
> **A person's actions can have many consequences.**
> **Rosa Parks's action changed American society.**

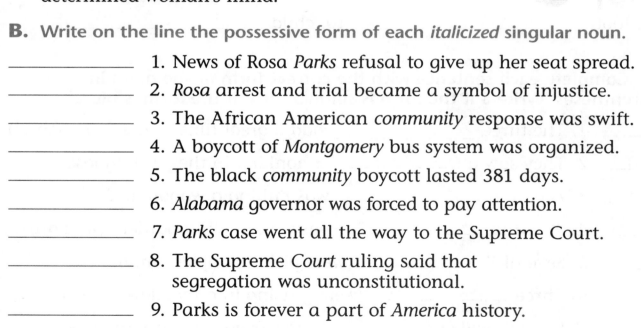

A. Underline the possessive noun in each sentence.

1. Rosa Parks's story began on December 1, 1955, on a public bus in Montgomery, Alabama.

2. A white man's demand for her seat on the bus upset her.

3. Rosa Parks's response to the man was a polite no.

4. The bus driver's reaction was to call the police.

5. Even being arrested couldn't change this determined woman's mind.

B. Write on the line the possessive form of each *italicized* singular noun.

_____ 1. News of Rosa *Parks* refusal to give up her seat spread.

_____ 2. *Rosa* arrest and trial became a symbol of injustice.

_____ 3. The African American *community* response was swift.

_____ 4. A boycott of *Montgomery* bus system was organized.

_____ 5. The black *community* boycott lasted 381 days.

_____ 6. *Alabama* governor was forced to pay attention.

_____ 7. *Parks* case went all the way to the Supreme Court.

_____ 8. The Supreme *Court* ruling said that segregation was unconstitutional.

_____ 9. Parks is forever a part of *America* history.

_____ 10. A *person* action in the cause of justice can indeed change people's lives.

Rosa Parks fought for equal treatment under the law for all people. Give an example of how you can work for fair and equal treatment for everyone.

22. More Singular Possessive Nouns

Underline the noun in each sentence that should be in singular possessive form. Write the possessive form on the line.

__America's__ **Most of America states have adopted an official bird, tree, and flower.**

_____ 1. Mom favorite bird is the cardinal, the Kentucky state bird.

_____ 2. The robin is Michigan state bird.

_____ 3. New York bluebird appears on a stamp.

_____ 4. Florida official bird is the mockingbird.

_____ 5. The southern pine is Arkansas official tree.

_____ 6. South Carolina official tree is the palmetto.

_____ 7. The hemlock adoptive state is Pennsylvania.

_____ 8. Illinois violet appears on travel brochures.

_____ 9. I have never seen Alabama official flower, the camellia.

_____ 10. Among Hawaii flowers is the hibiscus, the state flower.

_____ 11. California redwoods grow taller than you can imagine.

_____ 12. The dogwood white petals appear throughout Missouri in the spring.

_____ 13. The postcard from Tennessee showed the iris purple petals.

_____ 14. Dad love of the chickadee started when he moved to Massachusetts.

_____ 15. Sometimes a state official symbols are suggested by school children.

23. Plural Possessive Nouns

Nouns

> To form the **plural possessive** of a regular noun, add an apostrophe (') after the -s of the plural form (s'). When a plural noun is irregular—when the plural does not end in -s—add an apostrophe and s ('s).
>
> | | |
> |---|---|
> | SINGULAR NOUN | A circus <u>performer</u> must be physically fit. |
> | PLURAL NOUN | Circus <u>performers</u> travel around the country. |
> | PLURAL POSSESSIVE NOUN | Circus <u>performers'</u> lives must be interesting! |
> | SINGULAR NOUN | The <u>child</u> held the red balloon. |
> | PLURAL NOUN | The <u>children</u> held the balloons. |
> | PLURAL POSSESSIVE NOUN | The <u>children's</u> balloons were different colors. |

A. Complete the chart with the plural form and the plural possessive form of each singular noun.

	PLURAL	PLURAL POSSESSIVE	
1. ringmaster	_____	the _____	tall hats
2. lion tamer	_____	the _____	whips
3. clown	_____	the _____	smiles
4. trapeze artist	_____	the _____	nets
5. elephant	_____	the _____	trunks

B. Write on the line the possessive form of the italicized plural noun.

_____ 1. My *grandparents* surprise was a trip to the circus!

_____ 2. I loved seeing all the circus *performers* acts.

_____ 3. My older *brothers* favorites were the trained animals.

_____ 4. I preferred watching the *clowns* crazy stunts.

_____ 5. My grandparents enjoyed the *magicians* tricks.

24. More Plural Possessive Nouns

Underline the noun in each sentence that should be in plural possessive form. On the line write the plural possessive form.

____humans'____   **Two hundred years ago most humans homes were built from local materials found in nature.**

_____ 1. Tribes from the Great Plains made tepees walls from animal skins.

_____ 2. Many Native American tribes in the West used logs and mud for their homes walls.

_____ 3. For tribes east of the Mississippi River, women work might include building a wigwam.

_____ 4. Those shelters walls were often made of grass mats.

_____ 5. Pumpkins vitamins helped Native Americans and colonists survive hard winters.

_____ 6. Early European settlers may have made homes that looked like the local tribes wooden longhouses.

_____ 7. Food from Native Americans prevented many colonists deaths.

_____ 8. Foods such as potatoes and tomatoes were new to colonists, who did not always like the foods flavors.

_____ 9. Carrots colors could be yellow, red, orange, or purple.

_____ 10. For many years life in the colonies was too hard for settlers to care for oxen needs.

25. Collective Nouns

> A noun that names a group of things or people is called a **collective noun.** A collective noun is usually considered to be singular.
>
> **The scout <u>troop</u> camps in the woods every summer.**

A. Circle the collective noun in each sentence.

1. The whole class went to the concert.

2. The chorus marched onto the stage.

3. We waited for the orchestra to play.

4. Everyone in the audience loved the show.

5. A group of us went backstage to ask for autographs.

B. Complete each sentence with a collective noun. Use each of the nouns from the list once.

audience	crew	flock	litter	hive
club	family	herd	pack	team

1. The _____ on the sailboat raised the sails.

2. We saw a _____ of geese flying overhead.

3. The members of the music _____ raised money for new instruments.

4. The _____ of wolves howled at the moon.

5. My dog had a _____ of puppies.

6. Everyone on the _____ was happy about the victory.

7. A _____ of cattle ate grass in the field.

8. My grandfather keeps a _____ of bees.

9. Lydia and her _____ went to the beach.

10. Everyone in the _____ stood up and clapped.

26. Count Nouns and Noncount Nouns

Count nouns name things that exist as individual units. You can count them. A count noun has a singular and a plural form.

SINGULAR	PLURAL	SINGULAR	PLURAL
girl	**girls**	**tooth**	**teeth**

Noncount nouns name things that cannot be counted. A noncount noun has only a singular form.

   weather   **envy**   **rice**

Some nouns can be count or noncount nouns, depending on how they are used.

   They sell cakes at this bakery. Cake is my favorite dessert.

A. Write **C** if the noun is count or **N** if it is noncount.

1. milk _____   6. bird _____

2. meat _____   7. spaghetti _____

3. sister _____   8. porch _____

4. toaster _____   9. moonlight _____

5. joy _____   10. field _____

B. Circle each count noun and underline each noncount noun.

1. Our trip to the lake was a lot of fun.

2. My sister played in the water, and I made a castle in the sand.

3. My mom caught a fish while my dad set up the camping equipment.

4. We put our extra food and clothing in the tent.

5. For dinner we ate hotdogs and drank lemonade.

6. There were strawberries and ice cream for dessert.

7. As darkness fell, my dad built a fire.

8. We toasted marshmallows over the flames.

9. The peace and quiet of the forest was wonderful.

10. Everyone in the family enjoyed the weather.

27. Nouns as Subjects

A noun may be used as the subject of a sentence. The **subject** tells what the sentence is about. The subject tells who or what does something or is something.

> **Pollution affects our environment.**
> (*What* affects our environment?)

> **People pollute our air, land, and water.**
> (*Who* pollutes our air, land, and water?)

A. Find the subject by answering the question beside the sentence. Underline the subject.

1. Many factories release smoke.   *What* release smoke?

2. Smoke makes the air dirty.   *What* makes the air dirty?

3. People throw trash in empty lots.   *Who* throw trash?

4. Some farmers use harmful chemicals.   *Who* use chemicals?

5. Pollution hurts people and animals.   *What* hurts people and animals?

B. Underline the subject in each sentence. Write on the line whether it answers *who* or *what*.

1. The exhaust from cars pollutes the air.   _____

2. Chemicals in the rivers kill fish.   _____

3. Oil pollutes the ocean and marine life.   _____

4. Caring citizens clean up the environment.   _____

5. Laws can help protect our environment.   _____

Name _____

28. Nouns as Direct Objects

A noun may be used as the **direct object** of a sentence. The direct object tells whom or what receives the action of the verb.

> **People admire inventors.**
> (People admire *whom?*)
>
> **Alexander Graham Bell invented the first telephone.**
> (Alexander Graham Bell invented *what?*)

A. Find the direct object by answering the question beside each sentence. Underline the direct object.

1. Edison and Swan sold the first light bulb.   Edison and Swan sold *what?*

2. Fox designed the umbrella in 1874.   Fox designed *what?*

3. Mrs. Cockran made the first dishwasher.   Mrs. Cockran made *what?*

4. Raytheon created the microwave oven.   Raytheon created *what?*

5. Inventions help people.   Inventions help *whom?*

B. Underline the direct object in each sentence. Write on the line whether it answers the question *whom* or *what*.

1. Sometimes people wanted entertainment.   _____

2. In 1844 Sax invented the saxophone.   _____

3. In 1847 Ingram sold blow-up party balloons.   _____

4. Blackton produced the first animated cartoon.   _____

5. These inventions delighted young people.   _____

29. Nouns as Subject Complements

A **subject complement** gives information about the subject of a sentence. A subject complement follows a linking verb, such as the verb *be* and its various forms *(am, is, are, was, were)*. A noun used as a subject complement renames the subject of the sentence.

Brazil is the largest country in South America.
Brazil = country

A. Circle the subject complement in each sentence.

1. Pico da Neblina is Brazil's highest mountain.

2. The Amazon is the world's second longest river.

3. Iguaçu Falls is the world's widest waterfall.

4. Iguaçu National Park is the home of about 700 species of butterflies.

5. Duck is a favorite food in the Amazon region.

6. The official language of Brazil is Portuguese.

7. Carnival is the nation's biggest celebration.

8. Coffee is an important crop of Brazil.

9. Dom Pedro was once the emperor of Brazil.

10. Today Brazil is a republic.

B. Complete each sentence with a noun subject complement.

1. My favorite food is _____ .

2. My best subject in school is _____ .

3. My favorite birthday presents were _____ .

4. The best park in our town is _____ .

5. The biggest city in our state is _____ .

Nouns

Name _____

30. Reviewing Nouns

A. Underline each proper noun. Circle each common noun.

1. There are many kinds of natural disasters.
2. One famous natural disaster happened long ago, in AD 79.
3. Mount Vesuvius, a volcano in Italy, erupted.
4. The lava and ash from the volcano buried the city of Pompeii.
5. Archaeologists discovered the ruins of Pompeii and another city called Herculaneum in the 18th century.

B. Write **S** in the parentheses if the *italicized* noun is singular or **P** if it is plural.

6. Forest *fires* (   ) are another *kind* (   ) of natural *disaster* (   ).
7. *Trees* (   ) and *plants* (   ) in the *forest* (   ) dry out when there is not enough rain.
8. A single *bolt* (   ) of lightning can cause fires that destroy whole *forests* (   ).
9. The *flames* (   ) can also destroy animals and even houses in the *area* (   ).
10. In these *emergencies* (   ) firefighters spend *days* (   ) trying to put out the fire.

C. Complete each sentence with the possessive form of the singular or plural noun at the left.

hurricane   11. A _____ direction and speed can change quickly.

person   12. A _____ best protection in a tornado is to go into a storm shelter.

children   13. The _____ shoes were carried downstream by the flood.

experts   14. The _____ opinions on the force of the earthquake varied.

Earthquakes   15. _____ effects can be severe.

D. Underline the simple subject and circle the direct object(s) in each sentence.

16. Many people build homes in villages near volcanoes.

17. Volcanoes may destroy those homes.

18. People will risk the destruction of their homes for economic reasons.

19. The land's rich soil promises good crops for farmers.

20. A volcano's eruptions create new land and rich soil.

Try It Yourself

Imagine a bad storm in your town. Write four sentences about the storm. Include a simple subject in each sentence. Include at least one example of a direct object and one example of a possessive noun in your sentences.

_____

_____

_____

_____

Check Your Own Work

Choose a piece of writing from your portfolio, a work in progress, an assignment from another class, or a letter. Revise it, using the skills you have reviewed. This checklist will help you.

✔ Have you capitalized all proper nouns?

✔ Have you followed the rules you learned for plural nouns?

✔ Have you used the apostrophe correctly in possessive nouns?

31. Personal Pronouns

> A **personal pronoun** is a word that takes the place of a noun. The personal pronouns are *I, me, mine, we, us, ours, you, yours, she, her, hers, he, him, his, it, its, they, them,* and *theirs.*
>
> NOUN   **Who were the pioneers?**
>
> PRONOUN   **They were people who traveled to the American West.**

A. Underline the personal pronoun(s) in each sentence.

1. Where did they come from?
2. They came from the eastern states and from far away.
3. It was a long time ago, in the 19th century.
4. Mom told me that we had pioneers in the family.
5. One of them brought two cousins with him to Kansas.
6. He didn't bring a wife?
7. Well, not right away. She didn't want to come at first.
8. Did he finally convince her to come?
9. Yes. She brought the family dog with her too.
10. Well, I am sure he was happy to see them both!

B. In each pair of sentences, a pronoun is *italicized.* Circle the noun each pronoun refers to.

1. Pioneers had to plan their trip west very carefully.
   They had to take all necessary supplies with them.
2. Each pioneer family had a wagon.
   Everything had to fit into *it*.
3. The pioneers had to bring seeds.
   They needed *them* to grow food.
4. People had to bring tools to make furniture.
   They couldn't make *it* without tools.
5. Weapons were important too.
   If a man lost *them*, he couldn't hunt or defend himself.

32. First Person Pronouns

> A personal pronoun names the person speaking; the person spoken to; or the person, place, or thing spoken about. The personal pronouns that name the speaker are *I, me, mine, we, us,* and *ours.*
>
> **At our school, teachers and students enjoy field trips.**
> **At our school, we enjoy field trips.**

A. Circle the pronoun that names the person speaking in each sentence.

1. We went to see the new planetarium at the museum.

2. Our teacher showed us where to leave our coats and backpacks.

3. A special guide explained the tour to us.

4. I didn't know the solar system was so big.

5. We counted many moons around some of the planets.

6. The guide invited me to visit the planetarium again.

7. I will definitely come back someday.

8. We collected our things and went back to school.

9. I asked friends to name a favorite planet.

10. Mine is Saturn because of its many rings.

B. Complete each sentence with a pronoun that names the person speaking.

1. The teacher wants _____ to do reports on the planets.

2. _____ want to report on the planet Saturn, and so does Toshi.

3. _____ will work together on our report.

4. _____ want to talk about Titan, one of Saturn's moons.

5. Titan is interesting to _____ because it is the biggest moon, bigger than the planet Mercury!

33. Second Person Pronouns

> The personal pronouns that name the person or persons spoken
> to are *you* and *yours*. *You* and *yours* can be either singular or plural.
>
> **Would <u>you</u> like something to eat?**

A. Circle the pronouns that name the person(s) spoken to
in the sentences.

1. How do you know that you are hungry?

2. By growling, your stomach tells you that it's time to eat.

3. You also know that it's time to eat when you feel shaky or tired.

4. You need to eat about every four hours during the day.

5. After you eat, the process of digestion begins.

6. You begin to digest food in your mouth, where saliva makes it soft.

7. The food you have chewed and softened goes down the esophagus.

8. Your stomach then breaks down the food into a liquid so that you
   can receive its nutrients.

9. The nutrients in the food give you energy.

10. Carrots might give you energy between meals.

B. Write an **F** on the line if the pronoun in *italics*
is a first person pronoun. Write an **S** if the pronoun
is a second person pronoun.

_____ 1. *I* have a bright orange umbrella
with green dots.

_____ 2. *Yours* has cartoon characters on it.

_____ 3. This umbrella is so big that *we*
can both fit under it!

_____ 4. These raincoats belong to *us*.

_____ 5. Would anyone like to wear
mine today?

34. Third Person Pronouns

The personal pronouns that name the person(s), place(s), or thing(s) spoken about are *she, her, hers, he, him, his, it, its, they, them,* and *theirs.*

When brave people see injustice, they work hard to stop it.

Circle the pronouns that name the person(s) or thing(s) spoken about in each example.

1. Harriet Tubman was born in Maryland in 1821. She was a slave who escaped to freedom.

2. Harriet Tubman knew that other people wanted to be free, so she decided to help them.

3. She made more than 15 trips to the South.

4. Harriet Tubman made very careful plans so that nothing would happen to her or to the people she was helping.

5. When people asked her for help, she guided them on the risky journey.

6. Hers was dangerous work, but she had bravery and intelligence.

7. She told slaves about homes and churches where they could hide as they traveled to freedom.

8. The homes and churches were part of a secret route called the Underground Railroad, and many slaves soon knew about it.

9. She helped between 200 and 300 people escape from slavery.

10. During the Civil War she worked for the Union Army, helping it by working as a scout, a cook, and a nurse.

Harriet Tubman put herself in danger to help others lead better lives. Give an example of what you can do to help people lead better lives.

Pronouns

35. Singular Pronouns and Plural Pronouns

A **singular personal pronoun** refers to one person, place, or thing. The singular personal pronouns are *I, me, mine, you, yours, he, him, his, she, her, hers, it,* and *its.* A **plural personal pronoun** refers to more than one person, place, or thing. The plural personal pronouns are *we, us, ours, you, yours, they, them,* and *theirs.*

SINGULAR PERSONAL PRONOUN   **He is interested in animals.**

PLURAL PERSONAL PRONOUN   **Animals are important to us in many ways.**

Circle the personal pronoun in each sentence. Write **S** on the line if it is singular and **P** if it is plural.

_____ 1. Some animals help us in strange ways.

_____ 2. One animal, the leech, looks like a worm, but it is quite different.

_____ 3. It has a mouth that acts as a suction cup.

_____ 4. A leech also has teeth and uses them to attach itself to another animal.

_____ 5. You might know that long ago doctors attached leeches to sick people to try to cure them.

_____ 6. They thought the leeches would suck out the sickness.

_____ 7. Doctors don't believe that anymore, but they are still interested in leeches because leech saliva stops blood from clotting.

_____ 8. Clotting helps us by stopping bleeding.

_____ 9. Some clots can be dangerous to you, however, because they can form inside the brain or the heart.

_____ 10. Learning how leeches can stop clots may help us prevent strokes and heart attacks.

36. Subject Pronouns

> A personal pronoun may be used as the subject of a sentence.
> Pronouns that are used as subjects are called **subject pronouns.**
> The subject pronouns are *I, we, you, he, she, it,* and *they.*
>
> | | |
> |---|---|
> | SIMPLE SUBJECT | **Magnets help us in many ways.** |
> | SUBJECT PRONOUN | **They improve our lives.** |

A. Underline the subject pronoun in each sentence.

1. Do you know much about magnets?

2. I learned about magnets in school.

3. They attract metal objects such as nails or paper clips.

4. We call this special attraction magnetism.

5. It is a valuable force that people can use in many ways.

6. In our kitchens we use magnets to hold messages on the refrigerators.

7. They are used in hospitals in special machines.

8. In maglev trains they keep the trains off the rails and in the air.

9. Did you know Earth is a magnet too?

10. It has north and south magnetic poles.

B. Write a sentence about the word or words on the left. Use a subject pronoun that takes the place of the word or words.

1. (magnets) _____

   _____

2. (Earth) _____

   _____

3. (your science teacher) _____

   _____

4. (you and your classmates) _____

   _____

5. (your science class) _____

   _____

37. Pronouns in Compound Subjects

> One or more subject pronouns can be used in a **compound subject.**
> They are connected by *and* or *or.*
>
> **Jacob and Kelly are riding their bikes.**
> **He and Kelly are riding their bikes.**
> **Jacob and she are riding their bikes.**
> **He and she are riding their bikes.**
>
> In speaking and writing, it is polite to put *I* after other subject words
> that name people.
>
> **She and I will ride our bikes later.**

A. Underline the compound subject in each sentence. Circle any subject pronouns.

1. My dad and I talked to my aunt last night.

2. He and she are planning my mom's birthday party.

3. My dad and I will go to her favorite restaurant.

4. My aunt and she will arrive a half-hour later.

5. The waiters and we will all shout, "Surprise!"

6. They and my dad will bring out a big birthday cake.

7. He and my aunt will give her their presents.

8. He and she will also give her some flowers.

9. He and I will each give her a big hug.

10. My family and I will sing "Happy Birthday."

B. Complete each sentence with a subject pronoun to make a compound subject.

1. My sister Sara and _____ visited my uncle in Boston.

2. _____ and _____ walked the Freedom Trail.

3. Sara and _____ sat in a pew in Old North Church.

4. My uncle and _____ rode in a Swan Boat.

5. _____ and _____ had a wonderful time!

38. Pronouns as Direct Objects

A personal pronoun may be used as the direct object in a sentence. Pronouns that are used as objects are called **object pronouns.** The object pronouns are *me, us, you, him, her, it,* and *them.*

DIRECT OBJECT (NOUN)	In the United States, citizens choose their <u>leaders.</u>
DIRECT OBJECT (PRONOUN)	They choose <u>them</u> through government elections.

A. Underline the object pronoun in each sentence except the *italicized* sentence.

1. *The election candidates stand on the platform.* We recognize them from TV.

2. They try to persuade us with speeches.

3. Posters and campaign buttons introduce them.

4. The reporters may interview you for a citizen's reaction to the speeches.

5. The candidates' promises interest me.

B. Write on the line an object pronoun that can take the place of the *italicized* words.

1. Many people don't trust *this politician.* _____

2. People want the truth, and some people think he doesn't tell *the truth.* _____

3. I didn't like his ideas, so I didn't watch *the politician* on TV. _____

4. As soon as the politician made his promise, he forgot *the promise.* _____

5. When the voters heard his speech, they trusted *the man* again. _____

39. Possessive Pronouns

> A **possessive pronoun** shows possession or ownership.
> The possessive pronouns are *mine, ours, yours, his, hers, its,* and *theirs.*
>
> **My favorite food is peanut butter. What's yours?**
> **Mine is tomato soup.**

A. Underline the possessive pronoun in each group of sentences.

1. Grandpa's favorite actor was Kermit the Frog. Who was Grandma's?

   Oh, hers was Julie Andrews.

2. We've seen many movies, and our favorite is *Chicken Run.*

   Really? Ours is too.

3. Which movie theater is your favorite?

   That new one on Spring Street is mine.

4. Their favorite snack at the movies is popcorn.

   Well, it's not ours; we like nachos.

5. Mom's favorite time to see a movie is in the evening. When is Dad's?

   His is in the afternoon.

B. Complete each sentence with the correct possessive pronoun.
The words in parentheses tell you which pronoun to use.

1. Gia and Howie entered their science project in a contest.

   _____ won second place! *(third person, plural)*

2. My rug project doesn't look anything like the Navajos' rugs do!

   Does _____? *(second person, singular)*

3. I always like Moira's paintings. She's really good.

   Yes. _____ are so colorful and full of energy. *(third person, singular)*

4. Look at the paper Ken and Judy made!

   Wow! It's a bigger piece than _____. *(first person, plural)*

5. Well, I'm no expert, but here's my clay pot.

   _____ is not finished yet. *(first person, singular)*

40. Possessive Adjectives

> **Possessive adjectives** are used before nouns to show possession.
> These adjectives are *my, our, your, his, her, its,* and *their.*
>
> **My backpack isn't large enough to hold all those books.**
> **Then you'll have to hold some of them in your arms.**

Circle the correct possessive word in the sentences below.

1. We listened to (their theirs) advice about the high water.

2. One of (my mine) goals had always been to canoe down that stretch of the river.

3. Today (mine my) buddy and I set off with a canoe.

4. There were others at the launch site, strapping on (their theirs) life vests.

5. We put (ours our) vests on, too, and shoved off.

6. We could feel the strong current and had (our ours) doubts about making this trip.

7. As we paddled, though, (ours our) fears were replaced by excitement.

8. (Yours Your) mind races with the thrill of paddling down that wild river.

9. We shot some rapids, and the frothing water nearly ripped (our ours) paddles away from us.

10. In the rapids all (yours your) thoughts must be on dodging rocks and boulders and staying upright.

11. We kept (ours our) craft upright but did take in some water.

12. I thought of my mom; (her hers) biggest fear was that we would capsize.

13. We had no mishaps on (our ours) trip, however.

14. I felt satisfied at having achieved (my mine) goal.

15. In (my mine) friend's opinion, we should come out and fight the rapids again tomorrow.

41. Pronouns and Antecedents

> An **antecedent** is the word that a pronoun replaces. A personal pronoun must agree with its antecedent in person—the person speaking; the person spoken to; or the person, place, or thing spoken about. It must agree with its antecedent in number—singular or plural. The pronouns *he, him,* and *his* refer to males. The pronouns *she, her,* and *hers* refer to females. The pronouns *it* and *its* refer to animals and things.
>
> **Laura is in the band. She plays the clarinet.**
> (third person, singular, female)
> **José plays the trumpet. Give him this music.**
> (third person, singular, male)
> **Those drums are ours.** (first person, plural)

Circle the personal pronoun in each sentence.
Underline its antecedent.

1. Lewis and Clark were traveling through the West, and they needed a guide.

2. The explorers met Sacagawea and asked the Shoshone woman to help them.

3. Sacagawea had just had a baby, but she agreed to go on the trip.

4. The baby rode in a boat, or he traveled on Sacagawea's back.

5. As the travelers crossed Missouri, they met a band of Shoshones.

6. The leader was Sacagawea's brother, whom she had not seen for five years.

7. Sacajawea asked her brother for help, and he sold the travelers some horses.

8. Captain Clark praised Sacagawea because she remembered old Shoshone trails.

9. Lewis and Clark's trip covered about 8,000 miles, and it took more than two years.

10. Sacagawea was helpful to the explorers, and they were grateful.

42. *I* and *Me*

> Use the word *I* to talk about yourself. *I* is used as the subject of a sentence. Use the word *me* to talk about yourself. *Me* is used after the verb as the direct object of a sentence.
>
> SUBJECT   **I am interested in snowshoeing.**
>
> DIRECT OBJECT   **It interests me.**

Complete each sentence with the pronoun *I* or *me*.

1. _____ love to camp and hike.

2. Last summer _____ camped in the woods of northern Wisconsin.

3. A good friend accompanied _____.

4. _____ had trouble staking my tent to the ground.

5. He helped _____ with the staking.

6. Later he challenged _____ to an eight-hour hike with him.

7. He and _____ had never hiked so long before.

8. After the hike he photographed _____ massaging my feet.

9. He also checked _____ for ticks.

10. _____ thanked him for that.

11. At night _____ sat by the campfire.

12. My friend joined _____ by the flames.

13. The crackling relaxed him and _____.

14. He informed _____ of another great trail to hike.

15. _____ listened with excitement.

43. *We* and *Us*

Use the word *we* to talk about yourself and at least one other person.
We is used as the subject of a sentence.
Use the word *us* to talk about yourself and at least one other person.
Us is used after the verb as the direct object of a sentence.

| SUBJECT | **We get sick.** |
| DIRECT OBJECT | **Doctors help us get better.** |

Complete each sentence with the pronoun *we* or *us*.

1. Why do _____ get sick?

2. Does something attack _____ inside our bodies?

3. Doctors examine _____ for viruses and harmful bacteria.

4. _____ can't see bacteria or viruses because they are extremely small.

5. To see them, _____ have to look through powerful microscopes.

6. _____ need to protect ourselves from these tiny beings.

7. Doctors can introduce _____ to the rules of good health.

8. To stay healthy, _____ need to eat well, exercise regularly, and get enough sleep.

9. These good habits help _____ stay strong and fight germs.

10. Sometimes _____ get sick anyway.

11. Something infects _____.

12. It sends _____ to bed.

13. _____ nurse ourselves back to health slowly.

14. The doctor warns _____ not to do too much activity too soon.

15. _____ are glad when we are healthy again.

44. Pronouns and Contractions

Pronouns

A **contraction** is formed by joining two words together. Personal pronouns can be joined with some verbs to form contractions. An apostrophe takes the place of the missing letter or letters.

ONE LETTER MISSING   **I'm**   (I <u>a</u>m)

TWO LETTERS MISSING   **we'll**   (we <u>wi</u>ll)

                                   they've (they <u>ha</u>ve)

On the line write a contraction in place of the *italicized* words in each sentence.

_____ 1. *I have* been reading about a woman named Dolores Fernandez Huerta.

_____ 2. *She is* recognized for working for the rights of women and workers.

_____ 3. Her mother said, "*She will* go to college," even though it was not common for Hispanic women to do so.

_____ 4. Dolores thought, "*I will* help farm workers earn better wages."

_____ 5. She said, "Their children need shoes, and *they are* hungry."

_____ 6. *She has* also helped other people who live and work in brutal conditions.

_____ 7. *We have* learned that she put herself in danger by marching in protests.

_____ 8. Huerta and another activist named César Chávez said, "*We will* form the United Farm Workers union."

_____ 9. Together *they will* be remembered for getting medical benefits and safer working conditions for farm workers.

_____ 10. *We are* inspired by her nonviolent ways of winning justice.

Dolores Fernandez Huerta has worked hard for social justice. Give an example of an injustice you would be willing to try to change.

45. Reviewing Pronouns

A. Circle the personal pronoun(s) in each sentence.

1. Most of us enjoy listening to or playing music.
2. I enjoy classical music, but my brother doesn't.
3. He likes to listen to popular music on the radio.
4. My sister and I like that music too, and classical music doesn't bother her.
5. What kind of music do you enjoy?

B. Write on the line what the *italicized* pronoun in each sentence names—the first person, the second person, or the third person.

6. *I* would like to learn more about folk music. _____
7. Did *you* know that every country has its own folk music?

   _____
8. Sometimes a traditional song is forgotten because people sing *it* less often than they sing new songs. _____
9. Some musical instruments are not played today because people lost interest in *them*. _____
10. *We* can learn about history by exploring traditional music.

    _____

C. Write **S** on the line if the *italicized* pronoun is singular or **P** if it is plural. Write **SP** above the *italicized* pronoun if it is a subject pronoun and **DO** if it is a direct object pronoun

_____ 11. You can take natural materials and use *them* to make music.

_____ 12. People can hollow out a log and beat *it* like a drum.

_____ 13. *They* can blow a shell to make a kind of trumpet sound.

_____ 14. *You* can fill a gourd with seeds or stones to make a rattle.

_____ 15. *I* know how to make a flute from bamboo.

CONTINUED

47

Pronouns

D. Circle the possessive pronouns in the sentences below.

16. I wish I had a voice like yours.

17. Mine squeaks and cracks when I sing.

18. Many singers take voice lessons to train theirs.

19. Hers is the softest voice I have ever heard.

20. His, so loud and booming, can be heard clearly from the back of the music hall.

Try It Yourself
Write four sentences about your possessions and your family's possessions. Use possessive pronouns.

_____

_____

_____

_____

Check Your Own Work
Choose a piece of writing from your portfolio, a work in progress, an assignment from another class, or a letter. Revise it, using the skills you have learned. This checklist will help you.

✔ Have you chosen the correct subject pronouns and direct object pronouns to replace nouns?

✔ Were you careful when you used singular and plural pronouns?

✔ Have you used possessive pronouns and possessive adjectives correctly?

✔ Do the pronouns match their antecedents in person and number?

Name _____

46. Descriptive Adjectives

Adjectives are words that describe nouns. A **descriptive adjective** gives information about a noun. Some adjectives come before nouns.

Scientists are careful observers of the world around them. They use descriptive language to record what they see.

A. Underline each adjective. Circle the noun that is described.

1. The egg was found in the side of a rocky cliff.

2. The scientist dug out the large, heavy egg.

3. It had a brown, leathery shell.

4. The egg had several tiny cracks.

5. A dinosaur had laid the unusual egg.

B. Which adjectives from the list describe the words below on the left? Write them on the lines.

soft   breakable   white   loud   sour

glass   1. _____

siren   2. _____

fur   3. _____

lemon   4. _____

teeth   5. _____

C. Choose an animal. Write five adjectives to describe it.

Animal _____

1. _____   4. _____

2. _____   5. _____

3. _____

47. More Descriptive Adjectives

> Adjectives are words that describe nouns. They tell what kind.

A. Write a noun that could follow each pair of adjectives from a story.

1. old, evil _____

2. shy, beautiful _____

3. handsome, brave _____

4. dark, gloomy _____

5. long, dangerous _____

B. Underline the adjective(s) in each sentence.
Write on the line the sense that each adjective refers to.
The senses are *touch, taste, sight, smell,* and *hearing.*

_____ 1. The magician gave her a bitter liquid to drink.

_____ 2. The prince attacked with his shining sword.

_____ 3. The child stroked the dragon's cold and scaly head.

_____ 4. The damp, foul odor of the dungeon was everywhere.

_____ 5. The thundering hooves of many horses announced the soldiers' arrival.

C. Think about a favorite story of yours. Describe some of the people and actions in the story. Use adjectives that refer to the senses.

Name of story _____

1. _____

2. _____

3. _____

4. _____

5. _____

Adjectives

48. Proper Adjectives

Some adjectives are formed from proper nouns. These adjectives are called **proper adjectives**. All other adjectives are called **common adjectives**. A proper adjective begins with a capital letter.

PROPER NOUN **France is famous for its many types of cheese.**
PROPER ADJECTIVE **French cheese is exported to other countries.**

A. Underline the proper adjective in each sentence.
Circle the noun it describes.

1. In many countries Swiss watches are a popular product.

2. People all over the world eat Valencia oranges from Spain.

3. We put Italian oil on the salad.

4. Our school uses Japanese computers.

5. I eat Thai food every week.

B. Complete each sentence with a proper adjective formed from the proper noun on the left. Use a dictionary if necessary.

Korea   1. Does your uncle make _____ barbeque?

Poland   2. We enjoy cooking _____ sausage outside on the grill.

Alaska   3. That restaurant is well known for its _____ crab dishes.

Belgium   4. _____ chocolate is some of the finest in the world.

Sweden   5. One of my favorite dishes is _____ meatballs.

France   6. _____ fries may have been invented in Belgium.

Russia   7. I poured _____ dressing on my salad.

Cuba   8. That restaurant serves the best _____ pork sandwiches.

Peru   9. Have you tasted my mother's _____ cooking?

India   10. Curry is an ingredient in some _____ dishes.

Adjectives

49. Articles

> *A, an,* and *the* point out nouns. They are called **articles**.
>
> INDEFINITE **St. Louis sits on a major waterway.**
>
> DEFINITE **St. Louis is one of the largest cities in Missouri.**

A. Underline each article. Circle the noun each article points out.

1. Long ago St. Louis was a little city near the place where two important rivers came together.

2. People traveled to St. Louis by boat on the Mississippi River.

3. These people brought goods to sell to settlers for a profit.

4. A family going west would stop to rest in St. Louis before the big move.

5. An expedition of explorers would stop to get necessary supplies.

6. By the 1840s St. Louis was known as the Gateway to the West.

7. The Mississippi River is still a busy route that helps the city grow.

8. Today St. Louis has many railroad lines and a large airport.

9. A vacation in St. Louis is an experience you will not forget.

10. If you take a trip to the city, be sure to visit the Gateway Arch, a reminder of the early pioneer days.

B. Complete each sentence with *a* or *an.*

1. St. Louis offers _____ lot of activities.

2. You can have _____ adventure every week.

3. Faust Park has _____ historic carousel and costumed guides.

4. _____ Earth Day festival is also held every year.

5. You can go on _____ steamboat ride on the Mississippi.

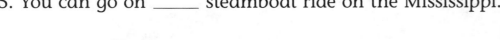

50. Demonstrative Adjectives

This, that, these, and *those* are **demonstrative adjectives**.
They point out specific persons, places, or things.
This and *that* point out one person, place, or thing.
These and *those* point out more than one person, place, or thing.
This and *these* point out persons, places, and things that are close.
That and *those* point out persons, places, and things that are far.

ONE, NEAR   Let's go to this living-history museum.
MORE THAN ONE, FAR   I want to see those examples of life in early
                                        America.

A. Underline the demonstrative adjective in each sentence.
Write on the line whether it points out one or more than
one person, place, or thing.

_____ 1. In this living-history museum, people act out
the lives of Pilgrims.

_____ 2. We can see what living in that time was like.

_____ 3. The floors of those one-room houses were made of dirt.

_____ 4. Pilgrim women made butter in these churns.

_____ 5. Life is easier in this century, don't you think?

B. Circle the correct demonstrative adjective in parentheses.
On the line write whether the noun is near or far.

_____ 1. In (this those) days Pilgrim children did a lot of work.

_____ 2. The sons helped their fathers in the
fields with (these that) tools.

_____ 3. Daughters helped their mothers cook
food in (these this) kinds of kettles.

_____ 4. In (those that) period, children didn't
have as many toys as they do today.

_____ 5. Would you rather live in (this those)
time or way back then?

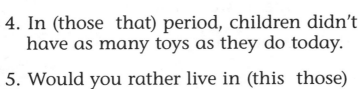
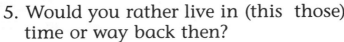

51. Adjectives That Tell How Many

Some adjectives tell exactly how many or about how many. These include words such as *one, thirty, several, few, many,* and *some.*

ABOUT HOW MANY   **Scientists use some measurements to tell about how many.**

EXACTLY HOW MANY   **Rarely do they say exactly how many based on only one guess.**

A. Complete each sentence with an adjective that tells exactly or about how many. The words at the left will help you choose an adjective.

exactly   1. Twelve inches equals _____ foot.

about   2. _____ countries don't use the metric system.

about   3. Touching the wires together caused _____ sparks.

exactly   4. If I have a dozen eggs, I have exactly _____ eggs.

about   5. I need a _____ more inches of copper wire.

about   6. The explosion created _____ shock waves.

exactly   7. A yard measures _____ feet.

exactly   8. I need _____ more quart to make up the gallon.

exactly   9. There are _____ ounces in one pound.

about   10. The universe probably has _____ planets.

B. Underline the adjectives. Write on the line whether each adjective tells *exactly how many* or *about how many.*

_____ 1. Seven beakers were lined up.

_____ 2. Some microscopes were delivered.

_____ 3. Several experiments were repeated.

_____ 4. We need five calculators.

_____ 5. Few test tubes are left.

52. Subject Complements

> A **subject complement** gives information about the subject of a sentence. A subject complement follows a linking verb, such as the verb *be* and its various forms *(am, is, are, was, were)*. An adjective can be used as a subject complement.
>
> **Harry Potter was very <u>brave</u>.**

A. Underline the subject of each sentence. Circle the subject complement.

1. Professor Dumbledore was tall.

2. Hermione is clever.

3. Ron's hair is bright red.

4. Hagrid is huge.

5. Professor Lupin's voice was hoarse.

6. Voldemort's second body was skeletally thin.

7. Harry's owl is very intelligent.

8. Quidditch can be quite dangerous.

9. Fluffy's teeth were extremely sharp.

10. The waters around Azkaban are icy.

B. Complete each sentence with an adjective used as a subject complement.

1. Skateboarding can be _____.

2. Popcorn is _____.

3. Roller coasters are _____.

4. Mosquitoes are _____.

5. Thunderstorms are _____.

Adjectives

53. Adjectives That Compare

Adjectives can be used to make comparisons. To compare two people, places, or things, the ending -er may be added to an adjective. To compare three or more people, places, or things, the ending -est may be added to an adjective.

ONE PERSON	**Maria is tall.**
TWO PEOPLE	**Ryan is taller than Maria.**
THREE OR MORE PEOPLE	**Chris is the tallest person in our class.**

If an adjective ends in *e,* drop the *e* and add the ending. If an adjective ends in *y* following a consonant, change the *y* to *i* and add the ending. If an adjective ends in a single consonant following a single vowel, double the consonant and add the ending.

The brown puppy is cuter than the black one.
It's also furrier than the black one.
It's the biggest puppy in the litter.

Underline the adjective that compares in each sentence.

1. Gertrude Ederle was the youngest person to set a world record for swimming.

2. At 14 she won an international swim meet by swimming faster than 51 other women.

3. At 19 she faced her biggest challenge—swimming across the English Channel from France to England.

4. The young American's time of 14 hours and 31 minutes beat the time of the speediest male swimmer by almost 2 hours.

5. When Gertrude returned to New York, two million people cheered for their newest sports hero.

Gertrude Ederle never stopped believing that she could reach her goal. Give an example of how you can stay strong and reach your goal.

Adjectives

54. Irregular Adjectives That Compare

Some adjectives that compare are not formed by adding *-er* or *-est*. They are **irregular adjectives.** Two common irregular adjectives are *good* and *bad*.

GOOD: TWO THINGS	The weather is <u>better</u> today than yesterday.
GOOD: THREE OR MORE THINGS	This sunshine is the <u>best</u> weather we have had all month.
BAD: TWO THINGS	This storm is <u>worse</u> than last month's storm.
BAD: THREE OR MORE THINGS	This storm is the <u>worst</u> one I have seen.

Adjectives

Choose the correct adjective to complete each sentence.

good   better   best

1. People have always wanted to control the climate and make their weather _____ than before.

2. One _____ solution is to live where you already like the climate.

3. Many people cannot move to a _____ climate, so they just try their best to feel more comfortable where they are.

4. In hot climates it is a _____ idea to wear light clothes and stay in the shade.

5. In very hot climates the _____ solution is air conditioning!

bad   worse   worst

6. A _____ drought can make farming difficult.

7. Heavy rains can make growing conditions _____ than before.

8. Extremely high temperatures create _____ conditions for plants, animals, and people.

9. Heavy snow and ice may be the _____ conditions of all.

10. Most people think a frigid climate is _____ than a tropical climate.

55. *More, Most*

Some adjectives that compare use *more* and *most. More* and *most* are used with most adjectives of three or more syllables and some adjectives of two syllables. *More* is used in comparing two people, places, or things. *Most* is used in comparing three or more people, places, or things.

ADJECTIVE	COMPARE TWO THINGS	COMPARE THREE OR MORE THINGS
delicious	more delicious	most delicious
unusual	more unusual	most unusual

A. Underline the adjective that compares in each sentence.

1. Mrs. Corelli has the most beautiful garden in town.

2. No one is more serious about gardening than she is.

3. Her roses are more fragrant than anyone else's.

4. The dahlias are the most colorful flowers in her garden.

5. It is the most gorgeous place I know.

B. Circle the correct adjective that compares in each sentence.

1. The acrobats were (more limber most limber) than the bareback riders.

2. The bareback riders wore the (more splendid most splendid) costumes of all.

3. The elephant was the (more enormous most enormous) animal there.

4. The tightrope walker was the (more cautious most cautious) performer.

5. The clowns were (more comical most comical) than the animal trainers.

6. The animal trainers were the (more patient most patient) people in the show.

7. The lions seemed (more ferocious most ferocious) than the tigers.

8. The (more bashful most bashful) animal in the show was a white pony.

9. The ringleader wore clothes that were (more formal most formal) than those of the other performers.

10. It was the (more outstanding most outstanding) circus I've ever seen!

56. *Less, Least* and *Fewer, Fewest*

> The comparative adjectives *fewer* and *fewest* are used with plural count nouns. *Less* and *least* are used with noncount nouns.
>
> **Anita bought less fruit than Charles did.**
> **Jay bought the least fruit of all.**
>
> **Anita bought fewer apples than Charles did.**
> **Jay bought the fewest apples of all.**

A. Write *count* or *noncount* after each noun. Then write phrases with *fewer* and *fewest* or *less* and *least*.

NOUN	COUNT OR NONCOUNT?	FEWER, FEWEST OR LESS, LEAST?
EXAMPLE **bikes**	count	fewer bikes, fewest bikes
1. chair		
2. furniture		
3. traffic		
4. car		
5. bus		

Adjectives

B. Write *less, least, fewer,* or *fewest* to complete each sentence.

1. Westlake Farm has _____ land than Briar Hill Farm has.

2. Briar Hill Farm has _____ animals than Pine Tree Farm has.

3. Pine Tree Farm has the _____ chickens of all the farms.

4. The _____ cows are raised on Westlake Farm.

5. There are _____ goats than sheep at Pine Tree Farm.

6. Westlake Farm raises the _____ corn in the county.

7. Last year the _____ wheat was harvested at Briar Hill Farm.

8. Briar Hill Farm has _____ heavy equipment than Pine Tree Farm has.

9. _____ people live at Pine Tree Farm than at Westlake Farm.

10. Briar Hill Farm uses _____ fertilizer than Westlake Farm uses.

57. Position of Adjectives

Many descriptive adjectives come before nouns. Adjectives used as subject complements, however, come after the nouns they describe. These adjectives come after linking verbs, such as the verb *be* and its various forms.

BEFORE A NOUN   **The <u>tiny</u> goblin sat on a toadstool.**

AFTER A LINKING VERB   **Goblins are <u>imaginary</u>.**

Circle the descriptive adjective in each sentence. Write B if it comes before a noun. Write SC if it is a subject complement.

_____ 1. Goblins are very scary.

_____ 2. They are creepy creatures.

_____ 3. They have sharp nails.

_____ 4. Their skin is green.

_____ 5. Their odor is disgusting.

_____ 6 Goblins like to play practical jokes

_____ 7. They are truly sneaky.

_____ 8. They put sour milk in your glass.

_____ 9. They steal your favorite toys.

_____ 10. They give people bad dreams.

_____ 11. Goblins can be nasty.

_____ 12. They prefer shadowy places.

_____ 13 They lurk in the basements of old buildings.

_____ 14. Sometimes they hide in thick bushes.

_____ 15. Goblins are always hungry.

Adjectives

Name _____

58. Reviewing Adjectives

A. Complete each sentence with *a, an,* or *the.*
Circle the proper adjectives.

1. California has _____ large number of people of Mexican ancestry.

2. It also has one of _____ largest Chinese communities outside Asia.

3. _____ English sea captain Sir Francis Drake claimed California for England.

4. Before California was a state, _____ Spanish ruled the area.

5. It became _____ American state in 1850.

B. Complete each sentence with *this, that, these,* or *those.* The words at the left will help you choose the adjective.

one, near   6. _____ state seal is for California.

more than one, far   7. _____ pictures show gold ore.

one, far   8. _____ bird, the California quail, has become the state bird.

more than one, near   9. _____ redwood trees are magnificent.

one, near   10. _____ part of the coast is my favorite.

C. Complete each sentence with an adjective that tells exactly how many or about how many. The words at the left will help you choose an adjective.

about   11. _____ people came to California to find gold.

exactly   12. California has _____ place known for films— Hollywood!

about   13. In 1906 a big earthquake destroyed _____ buildings.

about   14. Disneyland has _____ kinds of rides.

exactly   15. California had _____ state capitals before Sacramento—San José, Vallejo, and Benicia.

61

D. Complete each sentence with the correct form of the adjective at the left.

large   16. California is one of the _____ producers of manufactured goods.

popular 17. The Golden Gate Bridge is one of the _____ symbols of the state of California.

bad   18. The air pollution in Los Angeles is _____ than it is in Sacramento.

beautiful 19. Do you think the mountains or the beaches are _____?

good   20. The _____ vacation I ever had was my trip to California.

Try It Yourself

What do you know about your state? Write four sentences describing things you like about it, using adjectives.

_____

_____

_____

_____

Check Your Own Work

Choose a piece of writing from your portfolio, a work in progress, an assignment from another class, or a letter. Revise it, using the skills you have reviewed. This checklist will help you.

✔ Have you chosen adjectives that paint a clear picture?

✔ Have you used articles correctly?

✔ Have you chosen the correct form of the adjectives for comparison?

Name _____

59. Action Verbs

Many verbs express action. **Action verbs** tell what someone or something does.

Our body parts <u>perform</u> many different jobs.

A. Underline the action verb(s) in each sentence.

1. The nose cleans the air we inhale.

2. The diaphragm forces air in and out of the lungs.

3. The vibration of the vocal cords produces sound.

4. The heart pumps blood throughout the body.

5. Blood carries oxygen and nutrients to all parts of the body.

6. Cells in the body fight infections.

7. The skin protects us from germs and infection.

8. Kidneys clean and filter the blood.

9. Tears from tear ducts wet and clean the eyes.

10. The teeth break food into small pieces for digestion.

B. Look at the action verbs listed. Choose the one that completes each sentence and write it on the line.

    cool   controls   support   prevent   store

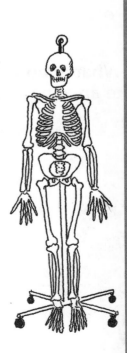

1. Our eyelashes _____ particles from hurting our eyes.

2. Our bones _____ our bodies.

3. The inner ear _____ our balance.

4. Sweat glands _____ our bodies when we are too hot.

5. The fat cells of our bodies _____ energy.

63

60. More Action Verbs

A. Complete each sentence with an action verb. Choose from the action verbs below. Each verb is used only once.

wish	**tastes**	**drink**	**spread**	**eat**
pour	**makes**	**buy**	**cuts**	**toasts**

1. Many people _____ milk at breakfast.

2. Sometimes they _____ it over their cereal.

3. My dad thinks milk _____ good in coffee or tea.

4. We _____ a gallon of milk at the grocery store every week.

5. For lunch we drink juice and _____ sandwiches.

6. My mother _____ a sandwich for me every day.

7. She _____ the bread.

8. I watch her _____ peanut butter and jelly on it.

9. Then she _____ the sandwich into four triangles.

10. My friends _____ their moms made sandwiches like that for them.

B. What actions can you do with the following objects? Write an action verb on each line.

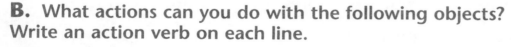

soap   1. _____   towel   6. _____

pen   2. _____   book   7. _____

oven   3. _____   crayon   8. _____

knife   4. _____   teakettle   9. _____

ball   5. _____   piano   10. _____

Verbs

61. Being Verbs

A **being verb** shows what someone or something is.
Being verbs do not express action. Some being verbs
are *am, is, are, was, were, has been, had been,*
have been, and *will be.*

There <u>are</u> many surprising special effects in space.

A. Circle the being verb in each sentence.

1. One special effect is a solar flare.

2. These bright flashes of light from the sun are
   electromagnetic radiation.

3. Another special effect is an eclipse.

4. There have been sightings of eclipses for centuries.

5. In a lunar eclipse the moon is in the earth's shadow.

6. In a solar eclipse the earth is in the moon's shadow.

7. In either case the result will be a large, dark circle in the sky.

8. The best special effects are auroras.

9. Auroras have been around for millions of years.

10. They are beautiful curtains of colored lights in the sky.

B. Underline the verb in each sentence. Write on the line **A** when
the verb expresses action and **B** when the verb expresses being.

_____ 1. Another special effect from space is a comet.

_____ 2. Comets are collections of minerals, dust,
gases, and ice particles.

_____ 3. Their glowing tails of dust, gas, and reflected
sunlight are millions of miles long.

_____ 4. Comets travel in orbits and in
regular cycles.

_____ 5. Halley's comet returns every 76 years,
for example.

Verbs

65

62. Linking Verbs

A being verb is often a **linking verb.** A linking verb joins the subject of a sentence to a noun, a pronoun, or an adjective. Some linking verbs are *am, is, are, was, were, has been, had been, have been,* and *will be.*

A. Underline the linking verb in each sentence.

1. My father has been a birder for many years.

2. It was he who took me on my first trip to watch birds.

3. Our location for watching was a beautiful redwood forest.

4. After we had been quiet for a long time, we saw something move!

5. It was a northern spotted owl.

B. Write on the line whether the *italicized* word is a noun, a pronoun, or an adjective. Underline the subject to which it is linked.

_____ 1. Many birds are *small.*

_____ 2. One of the biggest birds is the *emu.*

_____ 3. It is very *fast* and can run 30 miles per hour.

_____ 4. Years ago emus were almost *extinct,* but now they live in the wild and on farms.

_____ 5. These birds are *survivors.*

C. Complete each sentence with a linking verb.

1. Birds _____ the only animals covered with feathers.

2. There _____ about 9,000 types of birds on the planet.

3. The fastest bird _____ the peregrine falcon when it dives.

4. Some scientists think birds and dinosaurs _____ members of the same family a long time ago.

5. One day the answer to this question _____ clear.

63. Helping Verbs

A **helping verb** is always followed by a main verb. Some helping verbs are *am, is, are, was, were, be, being, been, shall, will, may, can, has, have, had, do, does, did, should, would, could,* and *must.*

At one time tulips <u>were</u> bought and sold like jewels.

A. A verb is *italicized* in each sentence. Write **LV** on the line if the verb in the sentence is a linking verb or **HV** if it is a helping verb.

_____ 1. Between 1634 and 1637, people in Holland *were* selling tulips for huge amounts of money.

_____ 2. Tulips *were* an obsession and a way to make a lot of money.

_____ 3. Rich people from many countries *were* anxious to collect the rarest and most unusual tulips.

_____ 4. A document *has been* found that shows that a man paid thousands of dollars' worth of animals, butter, cheese, furniture, clothes, and silver for a single tulip bulb!

_____ 5. After a while people got tired of tulips; the flowers *had been* just another fad.

B. Circle the linking verb or underline the helping verb in each sentence.

1. The agave plant has grown in Mexico for centuries.

2. It is a very useful plant.

3. Long ago people would use agave fibers as thread.

4. They could make a kind of needle from its sharp points.

5. Different parts of the plant were sources of food and drink.

Verbs

64. Verb Phrases

A **verb phrase** is made up of one or more helping verbs
and a main verb.

HELPING VERB   People **have** listened to stories for centuries.
MAIN VERB   People have <u>listened</u> to stories for centuries.
VERB PHRASE   People **have** <u>listened</u> to stories for centuries.

A. Underline the verb phrase in each sentence.
Circle the main verb.

1. Stories have been told around the world for centuries.

2. Stories have been used for different purposes.

3. They can teach us admirable behavior.

4. They can entertain us.

5. They can remind us of the past.

6. In most societies different kinds of
   stories are told.

7. Children have always enjoyed the adventures in fairy tales.

8. Other tales, called fables, have taught correct behavior
   through the moral of the story.

9. In pioneer days tall tales were created about extraordinary
   people and their impossible feats.

10. These funny stories would make people feel better during
    difficult times.

B. Complete each sentence with a helping verb. Two blank lines
mean that two helping verbs are needed.

1. In tall tales people _____ step over mountains
   and drink up rivers!

2. Children know they _____ hear a fairy tale when
   the storyteller begins with "Once upon a time."

3. Animals _____ always been the main characters in fables.

4. _____ you _____ reading any new stories?

5. If you tell me a story, then I _____ tell you one!

Verbs

65. Principal Verb Parts

There are four **principal parts** of a verb—**present, present participle, past,** and **past participle.**

The **present participle** is formed by adding *-ing* to the present form of the verb. The present participle is often used with a form of the helping verb *be,* such as *is, are, was,* or *were.* When a verb ends in *e,* form the present participle by dropping the final *e* and adding *-ing.* When a verb ends with a consonant following a vowel, form the present participle or past participle of the verb by doubling the consonant and add *-ing* or *-ed.*

The **past** and the **past participle** are formed by adding *-d* or *-ed* to the present. The past participle is used with a helping verb such as *has, have,* or *had.*

PRESENT	PRESENT PARTICIPLE	PAST	PAST PARTICIPLE
bake	(is, was) baking	baked	(has, have, had) baked
tap	(is, was) tapping	tapped	(has, have, had) tapped

Verbs

A. Write on the line which part (present, present participle, past, or past participle) of the verb is *italicized* in each sentence.

_____ 1. My family always has *liked* sports.

_____ 2. My mother *learned* to swim at an early age.

_____ 3. My father is *playing* in a golf tournament.

_____ 4. My brothers *love* to play soccer.

_____ 5. I have always *enjoyed* tennis.

B. For each sentence write the verb in the form given in *italics.*

1. I _____ fourth in softball this year. (bat, *past*)

2. You _____ two runs. (score, *past participle*)

3. She _____ the basketball to him.
   (pass, *present participle*)

4. He _____ it past the guard.
   (dribble, *present*)

5. She _____ the winning goal!
   (kick, *past participle*)

Name _____

66. Irregular Verbs

> The past and the past participle of a regular verb end in *-d* or *-ed*.
> The past and the past participle of an irregular verb are not formed
> that way. Irregular forms must be memorized.

A. Complete each sentence with the past or past participle form
of the irregular verb shown at the left.

write   1. Many authors have _____ about the Wright brothers.

go   2. I _____ to the library to check out a book about their lives.

be   3. The Wright brothers had _____ interested in the idea of
              flight since they were young.

draw   4. They _____ many designs for flying machines, some with
              engines and some without.

build   5. Orville and Wilbur Wright also _____ an early
              version of the wind tunnel.

fly   6. Orville Wright had _____ for 12 seconds on his first flight.

make   7. Orville and Wilbur _____ three more flights that day.

spend   8. By 1906 the Wright brothers had _____ more than an
              hour in the air on one flight.

grow   9. Interest in flying machines _____ quickly.

begin   10. By 1910 the Wright brothers had _____ their own
              company, called the American Wright Company.

B. Write in the chart the missing
form of each irregular verb.

PRESENT	PAST	PAST PARTICIPLE
1. blow	_____	blown
2. come	came	_____
3. _____	chose	chosen
4. do	did	_____
5. eat	_____	eaten

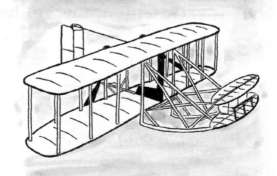

Verbs (side tab)

67. *Begin, Beginning, Began, Begun*

The principal parts of *begin* are as follows:

PRESENT	PRESENT PARTICIPLE	PAST	PAST PARTICIPLE
begin	**beginning**	**began**	**begun**

The present participle is always used with a helping verb such as *is, are, was,* or *were.*

The past participle is always used with a helping verb such as *has, have,* or *had.*

Complete each story with *beginning, began,* or *begun.* **Then guess whom or what the story is about. Use the names listed to help you.**

> **the Great Chicago Fire**   **John Wilkes Booth**   **Mount Vesuvius**
> **the *Titanic***   **the Boston Tea Party**

1. The iceberg that the ship hit was huge. The ship _____ to sink as water rushed in. People had _____ fighting for the lifeboats. **Story of _____**

2. The theater was full because President Lincoln was there. The play was _____. When people heard the shot, they _____ to scream. **Story of _____**

3. Smoke had _____ to come out of the top of the mountain a few weeks before. Fire, ash, and lava _____ to rain down. People and animals were trapped inside houses. **Story of _____**

4. Mrs. O'Leary's cow may have kicked over the lantern. Flames were _____ to spread out of the barn. The city's biggest disaster had _____. **Story of _____**

5. The patriots, masquerading as Native Americans, boarded the ships. They _____ throwing chests of tea into the harbor. A rebellion had _____. **Story of _____**

68. Know, Knowing, Knew, Known

> The principal parts of *know* are as follows:
>
> | PRESENT | PRESENT PARTICIPLE | PAST | PAST PARTICIPLE |
> | --- | --- | --- | --- |
> | **know** | **knowing** | **knew** | **known** |
>
> The verb *know* is not usually used in the progressive tenses. The past participle is always used with a helping verb such as *has, have,* or *had.*

Complete each sentence with *know, knew,* or *known.*

1. Long ago nobody _____ that the sun is the center of our solar system.

2. Today we _____ that the earth revolves around the sun.

3. People have _____ this since the time of Galileo.

4. Paul had _____ a lot about dinosaurs before he studied them in school.

5. In ancient times no one _____ anything about dinosaurs.

6. People today _____ many facts about those creatures.

7. At one time few people _____ that the earth is round.

8. Some people in ancient Greece had _____ that fact more than 2,500 years ago.

9. In modern times, people _____ that the earth is round.

10. Centuries ago people _____ nothing about germs.

11. Now we _____ that some germs can cause diseases.

12. Doctors have _____ this for many years.

13. Carol has _____ Lucy for two years.

14. She _____ when they met that they would be friends.

15. The girls _____ that it's fun to have good friends.

Verbs

Name _____

69. *Break, Breaking, Broke, Broken;*
Choose, Choosing, Chose, Chosen

The principal parts of *break* and *choose* are as follows:

PRESENT	PRESENT PARTICIPLE	PAST	PAST PARTICIPLE
break	breaking	broke	broken
choose	choosing	chose	chosen

The present participle is always used with a helping verb such as *is, are, was,* or *were.*
The past participle is always used with a helping verb such as *has, have,* or *had.*

A. Complete each sentence with *break, breaking, broke,* or *broken.*

1. The secret agent _____ the seal of the envelope containing his instructions.

2. He was _____ into enemy headquarters.

3. He needed to find out if the enemy had _____ the secret code.

4. Spies _____ secret codes all the time.

5. The enemy _____ the secret code just minutes before the agent arrived.

B. Complete each sentence with *choose, choosing, chose,* or *chosen.*

1. How do people _____ friends?

2. Some people have _____ friends because they are interested in the same things.

3. Some people have friends because someone _____ them!

4. When I am _____ a friend, I look for someone who makes me laugh.

5. I am glad you _____ me as your friend.

Verbs

70. *Do, Doing, Did, Done*

The principal parts of *do* are as follows:

PRESENT	PRESENT PARTICIPLE	PAST	PAST PARTICIPLE
do	**doing**	**did**	**done**

Note that *does* is a present form used with singular noun subjects and the pronouns *he, she,* and *it.*

The present participle is always used with a helping verb such as *is, are, was,* or *were.*

The past participle is always used with a helping verb such as *has, have,* or *had.*

Complete each sentence with *do, doing, did,* or *done.*

People often remember childhood songs, poems, and stories. One favorite story is *Miss Nelson Is Missing.*

Miss Nelson was a very sweet and patient teacher. Her students were not so sweet. They were _____ many bad things in class. They
        1
never _____ their work. Miss Nelson wondered what to _____. Then
        2   3
she knew.

The next day Miss Nelson's students had a new teacher. She wasn't sweet or patient. "What? You haven't _____ your work? What
                                                                4
will I _____ with you?" she would say.
        5

Many days passed. Now the students always _____ their
                                                              6
homework. They were _____ everything the teacher wanted them
                          7
to _____. They had not _____ anything bad in a long time.
      8   9
(Or anything fun, either!)

One day Miss Nelson came back. "Oh," said the students, "we missed you so much!"

"_____ you?" said Miss Nelson, looking very happy.
    10

Verbs

71. *Teach, Teaching, Taught, Taught*

The principal parts of teach are as follows:

PRESENT	PRESENT PARTICIPLE	PAST	PAST PARTICIPLE
teach	**teaching**	**taught**	**taught**

The present participle is always used with a helping verb such as *am, is, are, was,* or *were.*

The past participle is always used with a helping verb such as *has, have,* or *had.*

Complete each sentence with *teach, teaching,* or *taught.*

1. My aunt and uncle are musicians; they _____ music at Jefferson High.

2. Last year my uncle _____ my brother to play the clarinet.

3. This year he is _____ me.

4. First he _____ me how to read music.

5. Then he _____ me how to make a nice tone.

6. Now he is _____ me the fingering.

7. My mom and dad _____ at Jefferson High too.

8. They have _____ there for a long time.

9. My mom has _____ chemistry for two years.

10. Before that she _____ biology.

11. My dad can _____ math and physics.

12. They both _____ my brother and me a lot about science.

13. Right now they are _____ us the names of the stars.

14. They had _____ us the names of some constellations earlier.

15. I hope I will _____ science someday.

72. Simple Present Tense

The **simple present tense** tells about something that is always true or about an action that happens again and again. A verb in the simple present ends in -s if the subject is a singular noun or the pronoun *he, she,* or *it.* A verb in the simple present does not end in -s if the subject is plural.

A sea otter <u>lives</u> in the shallow waters at the edge of the ocean. Sea otters <u>spend</u> about eight hours a day diving and eating.

A. Circle the correct form of the present tense to complete the sentence.

1. Sea otters (sleep sleeps) in the sea.

2. A sea otter (wrap wraps) kelp around its body.

3. The seaweed (keep keeps) the otter in one place as it sleeps.

4. A sea otter (float floats) on its back at mealtime.

5. Its belly (serve serves) as a table.

6. Sea otters (eat eats) abalone, clams, and crabs.

7. Sea otters (use uses) tools.

8. An otter (open opens) a clam shell or an abalone shell with a sharp stone.

9. Sea otters (remain remains) playful animals, even as adults.

10. Oil spills sometimes (threaten threatens) the sea otters' habitat.

B. Complete each sentence with the correct form of the verb.

live   1. Beavers _____ in family groups.

weigh   2. An adult beaver _____ about 35 pounds.

slap   3. A beaver _____ its tail on the water to make a loud noise.

spend   4. These rodents _____ most of their time underwater.

build   5. They _____ large underwater lodges.

Verbs

Name _____

73. Simple Past Tense

The **simple past tense** tells about something that happened in the past.
Most past tense verbs end with -ed. If a verb ends in e, just add -d. If a
verb ends in y followed by a consonant, change the y to i and add -ed.
If a word ends in a consonant following a vowel, double the consonant
and add -ed. The past tense of irregular verbs does not end in -ed.

I **walked** my neighbor's dog.
The dog **tried** to get away.
It **tugged** at the leash.
We both **ran** down the street.

A. Write the simple past tense of each verb. Some of the verbs are
irregular. Check a dictionary if you need to.

1. bite _____   6. fly _____

2. curl _____   7. enjoy _____

3. make _____   8. carry _____

4. rake _____   9. ride _____

5. skip _____   10. jump _____

B. Complete each sentence with the simple past tense, using the verb
shown at the left. Some of the verbs are irregular.

go   1. I _____ to the animal shelter yesterday.

want   2. I _____ to get a kitten.

have   3. I _____ a hamster when I was little.

own   4. My mother _____ a cat as a child.

like   5. She _____ having a cat as a pet.

sleep   6. Her cat _____ on her bed.

brush   7. She _____ its fur every day.

give   8 She _____ it food and water.

teach   9. She even _____ it to walk on a leash.

help   10. Mom _____ me pick out my new pet.

Verbs

77

74. Future Tenses

The phrase *going to* and the word *will* are used to express something that will take place in the future. Both forms are used to talk about predictions or plans. To form the **future tense** with *going to*, use *am*, *is*, or *are* before *going to* and the present form of a verb after *going to*. *Going to* is often used to talk about an action that has already been planned. To form the future tense with *will*, use *will* before the present form of a verb. *Will* is often used when someone agrees to do something.

> We <u>are going to play</u> softball in the park.
> Harriet <u>will go</u> with us.

A. Rewrite each sentence in the future tense, using *will*.

1. Ben and his dad go to the recycling center on Saturday.

   _____

2. They put all their empty cans in a big plastic bag.

   _____

3. They tie piles of old newspapers with string.

   _____

4. Dad puts the recyclables in the trunk of the car.

   _____

5. They eat lunch on the way to the center.

   _____

B. Complete each sentence with the future tense, using *going to* and the verb shown at the left.

visit   1. My family _____ the Grand Canyon.

camp   2. We _____ on the South Rim.

join   3. My sister _____ the Junior Ranger program.

hike   4. My dad and I _____ the Bright Angel Trail.

try   5. My mom _____ horseback riding.

Verbs

75. Present Progressive Tense

> The **present progressive tense** tells what is happening now.
> The present progressive tense is formed with *am, is,* or *are* and
> the present participle.
>
> **The sun is shining.**

Complete each sentence with the present progressive
tense of the verb in parentheses.

1. My mother _____ me to the zoo. (drive)

2. I _____ my camera. (bring)

3. I _____ my friends by the ape house. (meet)

4. They _____ the newborn gorilla. (watch)

5. The elephant calf _____ right now. (feed)

6. We _____ to the large mammal house
   now. (go)

7. Elephants and giraffes _____ just feet
   from us. (stand)

8. People _____ peanuts to the elephants. (throw)

9. The giraffe _____ for my camera. (pose)

10. I _____ a picture of an extremely
    tall animal. (take)

11. My friends _____ the seals. (visit)

12. The seals _____ around in circles. (swim)

13. They _____ fish from the zookeeper. (eat)

14. We _____ at the noises the seals make. (laugh)

15. We _____ the zoo soon. (leave)

Verbs

76. Past Progressive Tense

> The **past progressive tense** tells what was happening in the past.
> The past progressive tense is formed with *was* or *were* and the
> present participle.
> **We <u>were laughing</u>.**

**Complete each sentence with the past progressive tense
of the verb in parentheses.**

1. Mom _____ the neighbors down the street. (visit)

2. They _____ a vegetable garden. (plant)

3. Dad _____ the paper. (read)

4. He _____ after a tiring day. (relax)

5. I _____ my homework. (do)

6. My brothers _____ outside. (play)

7. I _____ to their laughter. (listen)

8. They _____ fun. (have)

9. My whole family _____ out to dinner. (go)

10. We _____ at the family restaurant on
    Grant Street. (eat)

11. I _____ hungry. (become)

12. My brothers _____ on cookies. (snack)

13. They _____ their appetites for dinner. (ruin)

14. It _____ by dinnertime. (rain)

15. We _____ to the restaurant. (drive)

77. Present Perfect Tense

The **present perfect tense** tells about an action that happened at some indefinite time in the past or an action that started in the past and continues into the present. The present perfect tense is formed with *has* or *have* and the past participle of a verb.

> Melinda and her family <u>have lived</u> in New York since she was three.
> She <u>has sailed</u> her toy boat in Central Park.

A. For each example write the present perfect tense of the verb shown at the left. Some of the verbs are irregular.

sing	1. I _____	walk	6. she _____
kick	2. he _____	fly	7. it _____
cook	3. we _____	do	8. you _____
play	4. they _____	ask	9. I _____
jog	5. we _____	write	10. he _____

B. Complete each sentence with the present perfect tense, using the verb shown at the left. Some of the verbs are irregular.

go   1. Melinda _____ to Radio City Music Hall
            several times.

take   2. Her parents _____ her to the Bronx Zoo.

attend   3. Her mother _____ the Metropolitan Opera.

see   4. The family _____ exhibits at the Museum
            of Modern Art.

enjoy   5. They _____ living in New York City.

Verbs

78. Past Perfect Tense

The **past perfect tense** tells about an action that was finished before some other action in the past was finished. The past perfect tense is formed with *had* and the past participle of a verb.

I <u>had completed</u> my assignment before the bell rang.

A. For each example write the past perfect tense of the verb shown at the left. Some of the verbs are irregular.

swim   1. I _____

call   2. he _____

work   3. they _____

bite   4. it _____

crawl   5. we _____

run   6. she _____

give   7. we _____

tug   8. you _____

suspect 9. I _____

grown 10. it _____

B. Complete each sentence with the past perfect tense of the verb shown at the left. Some of the verbs are irregular.

see   1. Before Thomas Edison, not many people _____ an electric light.

hear   2. Until he invented the phonograph, nobody _____ recorded music.

work   3. As a teenager, Edison _____ on the railroad.

save   4. A stationmaster taught Edison how to work a telegraph machine after the teen _____ the man's toddler.

invent   5. Edison moved to New York after he _____ several new telegraph machines.

marry   6. Edison _____ his wife before setting up a workshop.

make   7. By 1879 Edison _____ an electric light bulb.

unveil   8. The phonograph became popular 10 years after Edison _____ it.

die   9. Edison remarried two years after his first wife _____.

become 10. By the time Edison died, he _____ famous.

Verbs

79. Future Perfect Tense

> The **future perfect tense** tells about an action that will have been completed by some future time. The future perfect tense is formed with *will have* and the past participle of a verb.
>
> **By June I <u>will have earned</u> enough money to buy a new skateboard.**

A. For each example write the future perfect tense of the verb shown at the left. Some of the verbs are irregular.

fly	1. she _____	bake	6. they _____
find	2. I _____	cut	7. he _____
print	3. we _____	help	8. you _____
rest	4. it _____	finish	9. she _____
plant	5. you _____	run	10. we _____

B. Complete each sentence with the future perfect tense of the verb shown at the left. Some of the verbs are irregular.

learn 1. By the end of the year, Mr. Ling's students _____ a lot.

read 2. By Christmas they _____ about the settlement of the West.

draw 3. They _____ maps of the Oregon Trail.

write 4. Marta _____ a report about the buffalo.

teach 5. By March, Mr. Ling _____ the class about the Aztecs.

build 6. Joey _____ a model of an Aztec pyramid.

paint 7. Jenna and Sam _____ a mural of the Aztec calendar.

taste 8. The class _____ some Aztec foods.

study 9. The students _____ the rain forest by May.

have 10. They _____ a successful year.

Verbs

83

80. Subject-Verb Agreement;
Is, Am, Are, Was, Were

A subject and a verb must always agree. A singular subject takes a verb such as *is, am,* or *was.* A plural subject takes a verb such as *are* or *were.* When the pronoun *you* is the subject, the verb *are* or *were* is used.

A. **Complete each sentence with** *is, am,* **or** *are.*

1. Did you know that chocolate _____ made from beans?

2. These beans _____ from the cacao plant.

3. The sugar and fat in chocolate _____ sources of energy.

4. I _____ crazy about chocolate.

5. _____ chocolate one of your favorite foods too?

B. **Complete each sentence with** *was* **or** *were.*

1. The cacao plant _____ known to people in Central America and South America more than 4,000 years ago.

2. Back then chocolate _____ a drink, not a candy.

3. Cacao beans and chocolate _____ carried to Europe by Hernán Cortés, the Spanish explorer.

4. Europeans _____ soon happily drinking chocolate.

5. It _____ in the 1800s that a Dutch scientist learned how to make chocolate into candy.

C. **Complete the sentences with** *is, am, are, was,* **or** *were.*

1. For a good dessert get some strawberries that _____ red and ripe.

2. After they _____ washed, ask an adult to help you heat some chocolate.

3. When the chocolate _____ soft and warm, carefully dip the strawberries into it.

4. Wait until the chocolate _____ cool, then eat and enjoy!

5. Now that _____ easy, don't you think?

Verbs

81. Subject-Verb Agreement; *Do* and *Does*

Do is used with plural nouns and the first person pronouns *I* and *we*. *Do* is also used with the second person pronoun *you* and the third person pronoun *they*. *Does* is used with singular nouns and the third person pronouns *he, she,* and *it*.

**Good students do several important things before they study.
Do you have good study habits?
Does your teacher explain the value of good study habits?**

A. Complete each sentence with *do* or *does.*

1. Some students _____ their homework promptly.

2. They often _____ a lot of reading or research.

3. My brother _____ his homework every day.

4. He _____ best in math and science.

5. I _____ best in art and music!

B. Circle the correct verb form.

1. Many students (do does) extra reading.

2. They (do does) their assignments promptly.

3. Lara (do does) research in the library.

4. She also (do does) research on the computer at home.

5. My brother (do does) physical exercise before homework.

6. My sisters (do does) their exercising after their homework is finished.

7. Many students (do does) not like homework.

8. They are afraid they will not (do does) well on it.

9. Most of the time they (do does) just fine.

10. (Do Does) you have homework tonight?

Verbs

82. *There Is* and *There Are*

> When a sentence starts with *there is, there are, there was,* or *there were,* the subject of the sentence follows the verb. The verb must agree with the subject.
>
> **There is a waiting list for the swimming class.**
> (*Waiting list* is the singular subject. It follows the verb *is.*)
>
> **There are many people on the waiting list.**
> (*People* is the plural subject. It follows the verb *are.*)

A. Circle the subject that follows the verb *is* or *are.* Write **S** on the line if the subject is singular or **P** if it is plural.

_____ 1. There are many objects in our solar system.

_____ 2. There is only one sun.

_____ 3. There are nine major planets that orbit the sun.

_____ 4. There are moons orbiting seven of the planets.

_____ 5. There are two planets with no moons—Mercury and Venus.

_____ 6. There are two kinds of planets—those made mostly of rock and those made of gases.

_____ 7. There are other things in the solar system too.

_____ 8. There is a special phenomenon called the solar wind.

_____ 9. There are many comets with long, dusty tails.

_____ 10. There is mostly just empty space, however.

B. Underline the subject that follows the verb in each sentence. Circle the correct verb in parentheses.

1. Long ago there (was were) strange ideas about the solar system.

2. There (was were) a man named Ptolemy who said Earth didn't move and that other parts of the solar system revolved around Earth.

3. There (was were) people who said Earth rested on a giant turtle.

4. There (was were) a belief that a giant dog took bites out of the moon during an eclipse.

5. There (was were) a society that believed Earth was flat.

Verbs

83. Reviewing Verbs

A. Write **A** on the line if the *italicized* verb in each sentence is an action verb or **B** if it is a being verb.

_____ 1. Sculptors *are* artists who make monuments and statues.

_____ 2. Some monuments and statues *help* us remember special people or important events in history.

_____ 3. Communities often *ask* sculptors to create big, important works to display in front of public buildings.

_____ 4. People *visit* a monument or statue and think about the person or event it pictures.

_____ 5. A monument or statue *is* a way to show respect for the past.

B. Underline the helping verb in each sentence. Circle the main verb.

6. Many monuments and statues are created as war memorials.

7. All around the United States, sculptors have made memorials for different wars.

8. One of the most famous memorials was installed in Washington, D.C.

9. A 21-year-old woman named Maya Lin had designed it.

10. This memorial has been known as the Vietnam Veterans Memorial.

C. Write **R** on the line if the *italicized* verb is regular or **I** if it is irregular.

_____ 11. Maya Lin *grew* up in Athens, Ohio, and finished high school there with excellent grades.

_____ 12. She was *accepted* to Yale University as an architecture student.

_____ 13. When she was a senior at Yale, she *heard* about the contest to design a monument to honor the soldiers who fought in Vietnam.

_____ 14. Many people were surprised that a young Chinese American woman had *won* the contest to design the memorial.

_____ 15. Some people did not *like* her design.

Verbs

D. Circle the correct verb form.

16. Maya Lin's design (is are) a plain V-shaped wall.

17. The stones in the wall (is are) black.

18. The carving on the wall (was were) not decorative.

19. It (was were) a simple list of more than 58,000 people who had died in the war.

20. Maya Lin (was were) upset about the criticism of her project.

 Maya Lin continued to work hard even when people didn't like her ideas. Give an example of when it is important not to give up.

Try It Yourself

If you were to build a monument or statue, whom or what would it be for? Why? What would it look like? Write four sentences about these things. Be sure to use action verbs and being verbs and to use helping verbs where necessary.

_____

_____

_____

_____

Check Your Own Work

Choose a piece of writing from your portfolio, a work in progress, an assignment from another class, or a letter. Revise it, using the skills you have reviewed. This checklist will help you.

✔ Have you formed the principal parts of regular and irregular verbs correctly?

✔ Have you used the correct tenses of verbs in your sentences?

✔ Do all of your subjects and verbs agree?

Verbs

Name _____

84. Adverbs of Time

An adverb tells more about a verb. An adverb can tell when, how often, or where. **Adverbs of time** answer the questions *when* or *how often*. Some adverbs of time are *again, always, early, immediately, now, often, sometimes, soon, then, today, tomorrow,* and *yesterday*.

WHEN?   **I will return the library book <u>tomorrow</u>.**
HOW OFTEN?   **I <u>often</u> read nonfiction books.**

A. Circle the adverbs that tell when or how often.

1. I will always remember the movie *Where the Red Fern Grows*.

2. Yesterday I went to the library for the book of the same title.

3. I found it immediately and began reading about Billy, the main character.

4. Billy frequently dreamed of owning his own hounds.

5. Early in the day he found a magazine with an ad for dogs.

6. First he had to save the money he needed.

7. Billy sometimes walked in the woods to think.

8. He often walked by a camp as he followed raccoon tracks.

9. He wondered again about buying the dogs.

10. Could he ever save 50 dollars?

B. Complete each sentence with an adverb of time from the list. Use each word once.

| daily | finally | frequently | never | tomorrow |

1. Billy worked _____ to earn the money for the hounds.

2. _____ he thought about the dogs.

3. Billy _____ bought candy while he was saving his money.

4. _____ the happy day arrived.

5. _____ Billy would chase raccoons with his two pups.

85. Adverbs of Place

Adverbs of place answer the question *where*. Some adverbs of place are *above, away, back, below, down, everywhere, far, forward, here, in, inside, near, outside, there, up,* and *within.*

WHERE?   **She had to go in just as the boys did.**
          What she saw inside really pleased her.

Circle the adverb that tells where in each sentence.

1. We reached the national park and drove inside.

2. We looked everywhere for animals!

3. There, in the trees, were at least three chimpanzees.

4. We could see a male baboon climbing up.

5. He began picking fruit and throwing it down to the ground.

6. We saw a large snake nearby, winding itself into a coil.

7. We stepped back to take photos of a pair of lions.

8. Some small antelope jumped forward as we approached them.

9. Colorful, noisy birds flew above as we drove by.

10. Some zebras moved away, trying to avoid us.

11. The warthog turned sideways and wouldn't let us photograph it.

12. We watched the river to see if there was a hippopotamus within.

13. We did get good pictures of a giraffe outside near our lodge.

14. We couldn't find an elephant anywhere.

15. The whole family agreed to come here again next year.

Adverbs and Conjunctions

86. Adverbs of Manner

Adverbs of manner answer the question *how*. Some adverbs of manner are *carefully, clearly, easily, gracefully, happily, kindly, quickly,* and *slowly*. Many adverbs end in *-ly*, but some—such as *fast, well,* and *hard*—do not.

How? **The science teacher closed the door quietly.**
She looked at the students quickly.

A. Circle the adverb that tells how in each sentence.

1. The students in the science lab were not working silently.

2. At table one, students yelled excitedly as two insects raced each other.

3. At table two, Roberto was carefully trying to stack three beakers.

4. At table three, students clapped each time the guinea pig curiously poked its head out of its cage.

5. At table four, Sarah and Hyun Jung were loudly reciting the names of elements from the periodic table.

6. At table five, Joanna was dreamily singing along to her headset.

7. At table six, Carl and Jack were happily tossing the globe of the world back and forth.

8. At table seven, students counted patiently to see how many times Jaehak could twirl his pencil.

9. At table eight, Butch was slowly pouring ink all over the science projects.

10. The new teacher awoke suddenly—it had all been just a bad dream!

B. Complete each sentence with an adverb of manner.
Use each word once.

attentively   neatly   politely   regularly   well

1. To do _____ in school, it is important to have good study habits.

2. Always listen _____ to the teacher.

3. Listen and then take notes _____ so that you can read them later on.

4. Raise your hand _____ to answer or to ask a question.

5. Review your class notes and assignments _____ .

Adverbs and Conjunctions

91

87. Kinds of Adverbs

Adverbs tell more about verbs. There are adverbs of time (*when?* or *how often?*), place (*where?*), and manner (*how?*).

ADVERB OF TIME (WHEN?)	The boys visited Aqua World <u>yesterday</u>.
ADVERB OF PLACE (WHERE?)	They want to go <u>there</u> again.
ADVERB OF MANNER (HOW?)	They left Aqua World <u>reluctantly</u>.

A. List each adverb in the correct column.

backward	early	forward	immediately	someday
cautiously	everywhere	gracefully	nearby	suddenly
curiously	expertly	inside	silently	weekly

TIME

1. _____
2. _____
3. _____
4. _____
5. _____

PLACE

6. _____
7. _____
8. _____
9. _____
10. _____

MANNER

11. _____
12. _____
13. _____
14. _____
15. _____

B. Complete each sentence with an appropriate adverb from the list.

1. The students _____ approached the glass wall.

2. Lateesha stared _____ into the water behind the glass.

3. Hundreds of fish swam _____ in the blue depths.

4. _____ she saw a huge gray shark.

5. It circled the tank slowly and then swam _____, opening its mouth.

6. Lateesha stepped _____ when it approached the glass.

7. Goosebumps appeared _____ on her arms!

8. Next she saw an octopus propel itself _____, toward the glass.

9. Then a huge eel left its hiding place _____.

10. What fascinating creatures to visit again _____!

88. Adverbs That Compare

Adverbs can compare the actions of two or more persons or things. To compare the actions of two persons or things, *-er* is often added to an adverb. To compare three or more actions, *-est* is often added to an adverb.

COMPARE ACTIONS OF TWO

Sandra swims faster than Gloria.
Peter lifts weights earlier than Ray does.

COMPARE ACTIONS OF THREE OR MORE

Of the three girls, Julia swims fastest.
Diego lifts weights earliest of all.

A. Circle the correct form of the adverb to complete the sentence.

1. Mary Lou swims (slower slowest) than Sue does.

2. Frank reacts (quicker quickest) of any player on the basketball team.

3. Kim's gymnastics routine was (longer longest) this year than her routine last year.

4. Of all the boys on the parallel bars, Geraldo landed (softer softest).

5. The crowd cheered (louder loudest) at this game than at the last one.

B. Complete each sentence with the correct form of an adverb from the list. Use each adverb once.

early   high   long   loud   slow

1. On our team Greta practiced _____ of all.

2. Tim jumped _____ than George did in the pole vault.

3. Of all the boys, Joe ran _____.

4. Ginny arrived at the meet _____ than Laura did.

5. Paco yelled _____ of all the sprinters when he won the race.

Adverbs and Conjunctions

89. More Adverbs That Compare

> Some adverbs that compare are not formed by adding -er or -est.
> Instead, these adverbs use *more* and *most* to make comparisons.
> *More* and *most* are used with adverbs ending in -ly and with
> adverbs of three or more syllables.
>
> | COMPARE ACTIONS OF TWO | COMPARE ACTIONS OF THREE OR MORE |
> |---|---|
> | She spoke <u>more calmly</u> than he did. | He worked <u>most diligently</u> of all. |

A. Underline the adverb that compares in each sentence.

1. The Carters work in their yard more frequently than the neighbors work in theirs.

2. Mrs. Carter grows roses most skillfully of all her relatives.

3. Mr. Carter waters their lawn more regularly than Mr. Davis waters his.

4. Jill works more tirelessly at pulling weeds than Jeremy does.

5. Jeremy prunes the bushes most carefully of all the Carters.

B. Circle the correct form to complete the sentence.

1. She types (more most) rapidly of all her classmates.

2. She works (more most) accurately than we do.

3. He tends to work (more most) carelessly than anyone else.

4. He behaves (more most) thoughtfully than many other students.

5. He shares his things (more most) generously of all the students.

C. Complete each sentence with the correct form of an adverb given.

frequently   1. The team is winning _____ than usual.

accurately   2. Juan is pitching _____ than he did last year.

aggressively 3. Luis runs the bases _____ of all the players.

smoothly   4. Chris swings his bat _____ than he used to.

fiercely   5. Marty wants to win _____ of all the players.

90. *Good* and *Well*; Negatives

The word *good* is an adjective. The word *well* is an adverb.

ADVERB   **Are you doing <u>well</u> in school?**

ADJECTIVE   **Yes, my grades are <u>good</u>.**

Use only one negative word in a sentence to express a negative idea.

What? You do <u>not</u> have any bad grades?
I have <u>never</u> had bad grades!

A. Complete each sentence with *good* or *well.*

1. Can he do this job _____?

   I'm sure he can. He is a _____ worker.

2. The new violinist is quite _____.

   He has been playing extremely _____ all night.

3. Some grapes grow _____ in hot, dry climates.

   California is a _____ place to grow them.

4. This knife doesn't cut _____.

   What you need is a _____ sharpener for it.

5. Your guest has very _____ manners.

   Yes, everyone speaks _____ of him.

B. Circle the correct word in parentheses to express a negative idea.

1. I have (ever never) seen you look so tired!

   Well, I didn't get (any no) sleep last night.

2. There's (no any) ice cream left!

   I know. I didn't get (any no), either.

3. Don't you have (any no) idea where the keys are?

   Sorry, I have (any no) idea at all.

4. Haven't you (never ever) forgotten your homework?

   Well, yes, but I (ever never) said the dog ate it!

5. Didn't the tuba (ever never) get fixed?

   I don't have (no any) idea what happened to it.

Adverbs and Conjunctions

91. Coordinating Conjunctions

The words *and, but,* and *or* are the **coordinating conjunctions.** They are used to join two words or groups of words that are similar.

Most boys and girls like amusement parks. (nouns)
Roller coasters are scary but fun. (adjectives)
You can see a show or play a game. (phrases)

A. Circle the coordinating conjunction in each sentence. Underline the words or phrases the conjunction joins.

1. Mom and Dad took us to an amusement park on Saturday.

2. The weather was sunny but cool.

3. We rode on the Screamer and the Whirlaway.

4. Clowns and acrobats entertained the crowd.

5. We could choose spaghetti or hamburgers for lunch.

6. You could eat in the restaurant or on the lawn.

7. Mom brought her camera and took pictures of everything.

8. We slid down a waterslide and into a pool.

9. We bought sweatshirts and hats.

10. At the end of the day we were tired but happy.

B. Complete each sentence with a coordinating conjunction that makes sense.

1. Penguin feathers are short _____ thick.

2. Penguins can swim _____ not fly.

3. Penguins eat fish _____ squid.

4. Penguins move on land by walking _____ by sliding.

5. Have you seen penguins in an aquarium _____ at a zoo?

92. Reviewing Adverbs

A. Underline the adverb in each sentence. Above the adverb write **T** if it is an adverb of time, **P** if of place, or **M** if of manner.

1. In the mid-1860s George Washington Carver was born in Diamond Grove, Missouri, and lived on a farm there.

2. Born into slavery, he was kidnapped as a baby and taken away to Arkansas.

3. Carver later returned to his place of birth.

4. He went to college in Iowa, where he did very well.

5. Carver studied hard and received a Master of Science degree in 1896.

6. He was hired by the Iowa State College of Agriculture and Mechanic Arts and worked there for the botany department.

7. Carver labored intensively to find new ways to use farm products.

8. His research was extremely useful.

9. He successfully developed hundreds of new products from peanuts, sweet potatoes, and pecans.

10. He eventually developed a substitute for rubber.

B. Underline the correct form of the adverb in parentheses.

11. George Washington Carver moved to Alabama and worked even (hard harder) than he had before.

12. He (more skillfully skillfully) developed more than 500 dyes and stains from nearly 30 different plants.

13. Even (more amazingly amazingly), he created substitutes for products as different as bleach, cheese, ink, sugar, and shoe polish!

14. Appreciation for Carver's valuable work grew (more steadily steadily).

15. President Franklin D. Roosevelt (rightfully more rightfully) chose to honor Carver with a national monument dedicated in 1943.

C. Complete each sentence with the correct word in parentheses.

(good, well) 16. George Washington Carver is a _____ example of achieving success through hard work.

(ever, never) 17. We should _____ forget to work hard and do our best.

(any, no) 18. Carver's story shows us that _____ challenge is too great.

(good, well) 19. His example serves us _____.

(any, no) 20. If you truly do your best, _____ circumstance can stand in your way.

George Washington Carver worked hard to overcome obstacles and gain success. Give an example of how you can work hard to find success.

Try It Yourself
Write three sentences about a parade you have watched or been in. Use adverbs of time, place, and manner. Use an adverb in a comparison.

_____

_____

_____

Check Your Own Work
Choose a piece of writing from your portfolio, a work in progress, an assignment from another class, or a letter. Revise it, using the skills you have reviewed. This checklist will help you.

✔ Have you chosen your adverbs of time, place, and manner carefully?

✔ Have you used the correct form of the adverb in comparisons?

✔ Have you used only one negative word in a sentence to express a negative idea?

93. Periods

A **period** (.) marks the end of a declarative sentence or an imperative sentence. A declarative sentence makes a statement. An imperative sentence gives a command.

DECLARATIVE   *The Crane Maiden* is one of my favorite books.
IMPERATIVE   **Read it to me, please.**

Write D on the line if a sentence is declarative or I if it is imperative.

_____ 1. The poor man whispered to the crane he had found and freed.

_____ 2. Later a young maiden asked the man and his wife for shelter.

_____ 3. They invited her to stay all winter.

_____ 4. She wished to repay the old couple's kindness.

_____ 5. Look for an illustration of the cloth she made for them.

_____ 6. Listen for the sounds the loom makes as the girl weaves.

_____ 7. She asked the couple not to watch her weave the fabric.

_____ 8. The curious old woman peeked through a crack in the door.

_____ 9. Find out what she saw.

_____ 10. Read *The Crane Maiden* by Miyoko Matsutani.

_____ 11. Matsutani also wrote *The Witch's Magic Cloth*.

_____ 12. This book is for little children.

_____ 13. Find it at the library.

_____ 14. Read it to your younger brothers and sisters.

_____ 15. They will enjoy this tale of an old woman and a witch.

94. Question Marks and Exclamation Points

A **question mark** (?) is used at the end of an interrogative sentence.
An interrogative sentence asks a question.
An **exclamation point** (!) is used at the end of an exclamatory sentence.
An exclamatory sentence expresses a strong or sudden feeling.

QUESTION MARK   **What's wrong?**

EXCLAMATION POINT   **Watch out!**

A. Place a question mark or an exclamation point
at the end of each sentence.

1. What did you say your last name was
   For the fifth time, it's Kubicki

2. You have a terrible memory
   I know, but what can I do

3. Did you know there are memory exercises
   You're kidding

4. You above all people should try them
   Do they really work

5. Come on, just try them and see
   OK, where can I find them

IMPROVING YOUR MEMORY

B. Write three exclamatory sentences and two interrogative
sentences. Use exclamation points and question marks.

1. _____

   _____

2. _____

   _____

3. _____

   _____

4. _____

   _____

5. _____

   _____

95. Capital Letters

> The first word in every sentence begins with a **capital letter.** Also use a capital letter to begin proper nouns such as the names of people, pets, streets, cities, states, countries, days, months, holidays, important documents, clubs, and societies.
>
> **My cousin Sarah was born in September.**

Use the proofreading symbol (≡) under the letters that should be capitalized.

1. benjamin franklin was one of america's Founding Fathers.

2. he was born in boston, massachusetts, in 1706.

3. he became a printer, learning from his brother james.

4. franklin moved to philadelphia.

5. in philadelphia franklin published *Poor Richard: An Almanac.*

6. he had three children: william, francis, and sarah.

7. he experimented with electricity and wrote the book *Experiments and Observations on Electricity.*

8. this book was published in london.

9. franklin traveled in europe, visiting england and france.

10. Later he became a member of the continental congress.

11. in 1776 he signed the declaration of independence.

12. the declaration of independence was an important part of united states history.

13. franklin also helped negotiate treaties with great britain and france.

14. late in his life he acted as president of the pennsylvania society for promoting the abolition of slavery.

15. franklin died in philadelphia in 1790.

 Benjamin Franklin gave his time to doing research and to helping his country develop. Give an example of a worthwhile activity that you can give your time to.

96. Titles of Works

Capitalize the first word, the last word, and each important word in a title. Do not capitalize a short word such as *the, of, to,* or *for* in a title unless it is the first or last word. A verb such as *is* or a pronoun such as *it* should be capitalized.

The title of a book or magazine is *italicized* when typed and underlined when handwritten. The title of a poem, story, or magazine article has quotation marks around it.

BOOK	***Owl Moon*** (or <u>Owl Moon</u>) by Jane Yolen
MAGAZINE	***Sports Illustrated for Kids*** (or <u>Sports Illustrated for Kids</u>)
POEM	"Casey at the Bat" by Ernest Lawrence Thayer

A. Write **B** for the title of a book or **P** for the title of a poem.

———— 1. "Celery" by Ogden Nash

———— 2. *Otis Spofford* by Beverly Cleary

———— 3. *The Phantom Tollbooth* by Norton Juster

———— 4. "The Owl and the Pussycat" by Edward Lear

———— 5. "The Lizard" by John Gardner

B. Rewrite each title correctly.

1. slow sloth's slow song by Jack Prelutsky (poem)

———————————————————————————

2. the incredible journey by Sheila Burnford (book)

———————————————————————————

3. time for kids (magazine)

———————————————————————————

4. the beasts of borneo by Sal Lupinski (article)

———————————————————————————

5. the ant and the grasshopper by Aesop (story)

———————————————————————————

97. Abbreviations

An **abbreviation** is a short form of a word. If a word is capitalized, its abbreviation is also capitalized. An abbreviation usually ends with a period.

WORD	ABBREVIATION	WORD	ABBREVIATION
Sunday	**Sun.**	**February**	**Feb.**
inch *or* **inches**	**in.**	**North**	**N.**

The abbreviations for metric measures and for postal abbreviations do not have periods. Postal abbreviations have two capital letters.

meter *or* **meters**	**m**	**Utah**	**UT**

A. Write the word each abbreviation stands for.
Use a dictionary if you need help.

1. Fri. _____

2. qt. _____

3. Ave. _____

4. NY _____

5. E. _____

6. Oct. _____

7. mi. _____

8. OR _____

9. Aug. _____

10. Sat. _____

B. Rewrite each example. Abbreviate each word in italics.

1. *West* Cornelia *Avenue*

_____

2. The play begins *Monday, January* 29.

_____

3. New Orleans, *Louisiana*

_____

4. Jay bought 10 *gallons* of paint.

_____

5. The kite had 50 *meters* of string.

_____

98. Personal Titles

Titles such as *Mr.*, *Mrs.*, *Ms.*, *Dr.*, *Sgt.*, and *Gov.* are abbreviations that go before people's names. Each title begins with a capital letter and ends with a period.

Mr. William Okungu   **Sgt. Laura Collins**

An initial is a capital letter followed by a period. A person may use an initial in place of a name. A country or an organization may use initials as its abbreviation.

Ulysses S. Grant   **C. S. Lewis**

Rewrite each name, using periods and capital letters where needed.

1. ms eileen collins   _____

2. gen dwight d eisenhower   _____

3. dr linus c pauling   _____

4. mr f murray abraham   _____

5. pres george w bush   _____

6. rep maxine waters   _____

7. rear adm grace m hopper   _____

8. sen joseph r biden   _____

9. mrs m f k fisher   _____

10. gov james h douglas   _____

11. dr mae c jemison   _____

12. u s senate   _____

13. rev john white   _____

14. ms j k rowling   _____

15. prof a dumbledore   _____

99. Commas—Part I

> A **comma** is used to separate words or groups of words. A comma is used to separate two sentences joined into a compound sentence. Commas are used to separate words in a series.
>
> **Maria, Sonia, and Kim were invited to our picnic at the beach.**

A. Add commas where needed in each group of sentences.

1. We bought ham bread and cheese.
   I put the ham and the cheese in a cooler and you carried the bread.

2. Mei-Mei brought insect repellent blankets and sunscreen.
   She also brought a radio but I forgot the batteries!

3. We had swim masks fins and snorkel tubes.
   Josh swam but you built a sandcastle.

4. We ran along the beach and we chased waves.
   We saw starfish crabs and fish.

5. I surfed but everyone else wanted to fish.
   Later we looked at postcards key chains and T-shirts.

B. Complete each sentence with words in a series. Add commas where needed.

(add nouns)   1. We brought _____ _____ and _____ for Kim's birthday.

(add verbs)   2. We _____ _____ and _____ at our friend's party.

(add adjectives)   3. We were _____ _____ and _____ after finishing all the food and games.

(add nouns)   4. Kim's favorite presents were the _____ _____ and _____.

(add nouns)   5. I hope I get _____ _____ and _____ for my birthday!

100. Commas—Part II

> **Commas** set off words in direct address from the rest of the sentence.
>
> **Karen, are you going to be a camp counselor again this summer?**
> **I don't know, Mark.**

A. Add a comma or commas to set off the word in direct address in each sentence.

1. Mark what about you?

2. Are you kidding Karen? Being a camp counselor is hard.

3. Mike turn off your alarm and get up!

4. Time to eat breakfast boys.

5. Campers remember to form a line.

6. Don't grab all the doughnuts Chris.

7. Stop crowding the little guys Howard.

8. Stevie what on earth are you eating?

9. Line up boys for today's hike.

10. Larry don't pack all that stuff; you won't be able to carry it.

11. OK kids what shall we sing as we hike along the trail?

12. Lenny save some water for later.

13. Where are your hiking boots DeShawn?

14. David do you have the compass?

15. Let's stop and have lunch campers!

B. Complete each sentence with a person's name in direct address. Use commas where necessary.

(a classmate's name)   1. _____ please lend me a pencil.

(a friend's name)   2. Let's meet after school to play _____.

(a family member's name) 3. _____ may I come with you?

(your teacher's name)   4. _____ could you repeat that, please?

(a team member's name)   5. Throw me the ball _____!

101. Commas—Part III

A comma is used after the word *yes* or *no* when it introduces a sentence.

Ann:	Do you want to play a game?
Bill:	Yes, let's play a guessing game!
Ann:	Let's see. I'm thinking of something in this classroom.
Bill:	Is it large?
Ann:	No, it isn't large.

Add a comma where needed in each sentence.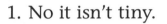

1. No it isn't tiny.

2. Yes it fits in a desk drawer.

3. No it isn't heavy.

4. No it isn't soft.

5. No it isn't expensive.

6. Yes every student has one.

7. No it doesn't have a sharp point.

8. No it isn't round.

9. Yes it can be made of wood.

10. No it isn't square.

11. Yes it can be made of plastic too.

12. Yes it has lines on it.

13. Yes it has numbers on it.

14. Yes you can measure with it.

15. What is the object? _____

102. Reviewing Commas

> Commas are used to separate words and groups of words so that they are easier to read and understand.

Put commas wherever they are needed in these sentences.

1. Class can you name a large North American predator?

2. Yes the grizzly bear is a large predator.

3. Grizzly bears can stand 7 feet tall and they weigh up to 1,000 pounds.

4. Their fur can be brown black red or blond.

5. A grizzly has a large head a long nose and a large hump on its shoulders.

6. Grizzlies eat plants roots berries fish small mammals and large insects.

7. During the winter they sleep in caves hollow logs or holes in the ground.

8. Grizzly cubs weigh less than a pound at birth but they grow quickly.

9. The cubs have short front claws and they can climb trees.

10. No male bears do not help care for the cubs.

11. In the summer Mr. Lee grizzlies eat up to 50 pounds of food a day.

12. Grizzlies are usually silent but they can make sounds.

13. They communicate with grunts growls roars or squeals.

14. In the United States grizzlies are found in Alaska Wyoming Montana Idaho and Washington.

15. Yes grizzlies are a threatened species and they should be protected.

103. Apostrophes in Possessives

An **apostrophe** can show ownership or possession. To show that one person owns something, place an apostrophe and -*s* ('s) after the singular noun. To show that more than one person owns something, place an apostrophe after the plural form of a regular noun. If a noun is irregular, form the plural possessive by adding an apostrophe and -*s* ('s) after the noun.

ONE OWNER	Joey's bicycle
MORE THAN ONE OWNER, REGULAR NOUN	the Murphys' dog
MORE THAN ONE OWNER, IRREGULAR NOUN	the children's newspaper routes

A. Write the singular possessive of each noun.

1. Miriam ————————————— friend

2. animal ————————————— behavior

3. Ms. Murphy ————————————— story

4. Joey ————————————— laughter

5. boy ————————————— route

6. neighbor ————————————— mother

7. woman ————————————— necklace

8. dog ————————————— fur

9. Max ————————————— bicycle

10. family ————————————— home

B. Write the plural possessive of each noun in the list.

1. actresses ———————————
2. bugs ———————————
3. cousins ———————————
4. grandchildren ———————————
5. horses ———————————

6. ladies ———————————
7. men ———————————
8. politicians ———————————
9. sheep ———————————
10. teachers ———————————

Punctuation and Capitalization

104. Apostrophes in Contractions

> An apostrophe marks the place where one or more letters have been left out in a contraction.
>
> | COMPLETE FORM | **I am** | **let us** |
> | CONTRACTED FORM | **I'm** | **let's** |

A. Write a contraction in place of the *italicized* word or words in each sentence.

_____ 1. *It is* too hot to stay here for our summer vacation.

_____ 2. I know! *Let us* go up north.

_____ 3. *What is* the temperature like there?

_____ 4. *I am* not sure, but the temperature will be cooler than it is here.

_____ 5. That *does not* matter.

_____ 6. *We are* never going to get tickets now.

_____ 7. *Do not* give up so easily!

_____ 8. Mom *should not* have trouble getting tickets on the Internet.

_____ 9. We *cannot* search the Web!

_____ 10. You mean the computer *is not* working?

B. Complete each sentence with a contraction that makes sense.

1. _____ you have any other ideas for our vacation?

2. Well, I have one idea that _____ cost us much money.

3. _____ that?

4. _____ just turn on the hose in the backyard and run through the water!

5. I hope _____ kidding!

105. Addresses

In an address capitalize the first letter of every title, word, and abbreviation. Capitalize both letters of a state's postal abbreviation.

Use a comma to separate an apartment number or a floor number from the street address and to separate the names of the city and the state. There is no comma between the state abbreviation and the ZIP Code. Put a period after every initial and every abbreviation except the state's postal abbreviation.

**Mrs. C. J. Wallace
395 W. Chicago Ave., Apt. 4A
Sheboygan, WI 53082**

Rewrite each address, using periods, commas, and capital letters where needed.

1. dr rogelio gonzalez
   346 w tijeras st apt 5C
   santa fe nm 87505

2. gen john c ryan
   2631 n lincoln blvd
   pierre sd 57501

3. ms keiko ito
   222 e parkside ave apt 121
   estes park co 80517

4. sgt karen l sanders
   528 river rd
   baton rouge la 79802

5. mr and mrs r h niles
   1854 e third st
   juneau ak 99811

106. Direct Quotations

> A **direct quotation** contains the exact words a person says. Quotation marks are used before and after the words of a direct quotation. A comma or commas are used to set off what is said from the rest of the sentence.
>
> **"I know a good joke," said Pat.**
> **Jim replied, "Let's hear it."**
> **"I hope," said Carla, "that it's funnier than your usual jokes."**

Add commas and quotation marks where needed.

1. I'll bet that you haven't heard this one Pat said.

2. We'll see replied Carla.

3. An elephant goes into an ice cream shop began Pat.

4. I want a large chocolate sundae said the elephant.

5. I'm sorry said the counter attendant but we don't serve elephants.

6. The elephant replied But it's hot outside, and I want a sundae.

7. I'll have to ask my boss said the attendant.

8. Tell her I want a super-sized sundae requested the hungry elephant.

9. My boss says I can serve you announced the attendant.

10. The elephant cried Great! Now make me that sundae, please.

11. Here you are, a super-sized sundae. That will be fifty dollars said the attendant.

12. You've got to be kidding! said the shocked elephant.

13. Hey, you're lucky to have it replied the attendant.

14. You know he continued we've never served an elephant before.

15. The elephant responded At these high prices, I'm not surprised.

Name _____

107. Reviewing Punctuation and Capitalization

A. Add periods where needed in each sentence.

1. I like to watch movies and read on weekends

2. This week I am reading about Gen George Washington

3. Prof Jensen lent me the book

4. It's called *George Washington's Teeth*

5. We saw it in a store on the corner of First Ave and Oak St

B. Write the abbreviations for the following words.
Add periods if needed.

6. Monday _____

7. September _____

8. North _____

9. Post Office _____

10. your state _____

C. Add commas and apostrophes where needed
in each sentence.

11. Yes the reptile house is my favorite part of the zoo.

12. I like seeing the turtles lizards and snakes.

13. Did you know that a turtles mouth has no teeth?

14. Mrs. Wolski can turtles eat flies?

15. Yes turtles meals can be insects or plants.

16. Some lizards can change color and some lizards can walk on water.

17. Snakes can live in water in trees or on land.

18. I like lizards but you prefer snakes.

19. Snakes eat small mammals insects and eggs.

20. I cant wait to visit the zoo again!

CONTINUED

Punctuation and Capitalization

D. Add quotation marks, exclamation points, and question marks.

21. Who was that mysterious girl

22. She said, I am Princess Charlotte of Windsor Castle.

23. What strange clothes she wore

24. I must be dreaming, said Terrie.

25. Was she really a princess

E. Use the proofreading symbol (≡) under letters that should be capitalized in each sentence.

26. terrie and her parents were spending the summer in chiswick, england.

27. each day mrs. wright took terrie to a place called kew botanic gardens.

28. terrie met princess charlotte there.

29. what strange thing did terrie discover at the museum near london?

30. you can find out if you read *the mysterious girl in the garden*.

Try It Yourself

Write three sentences about a trip you have been on. Punctuate correctly. Capitalize proper nouns. Include two contractions.

_____

_____

_____

Check Your Own Work

Choose a piece of writing from your portfolio, a work in progress, an assignment from another class, or a letter. Revise it, using the skills you have reviewed. This checklist will help you.

✔ Have you ended your sentences with the correct mark of punctuation?

✔ Have you followed the rules for commas and apostrophes?

✔ Have you used quotation marks before and after the exact words of a speaker?

✔ Have you capitalized all proper nouns?

108. Subjects, Verbs, and Direct Objects

A **diagram** shows how all the words in a sentence fit together. It highlights the most important words in a sentence and shows how the other words relate to them.

SENTENCE **Jeremy plays soccer.**

Start the diagram by drawing a horizontal line. Find the verb in the sentence and write it in the middle of the line. Find the subject and write it in front of the verb. Draw a vertical line between the subject and the verb. The vertical line should cut through the horizontal line.

Jeremy | plays

Now find the direct object in the sentence. Write the direct object on the horizontal line to the right of the verb. Draw a vertical line between the verb and the direct object. This line touches the horizontal line but does not cut through it.

Jeremy | plays | soccer

Diagram each of these sentences.

1. Cats drink water.

2. We ate dinner.

3. Amar watched television.

4. Karen made lemonade.

5. Horses eat oats.

6. They planted roses.

7. Bees make honey.

8. Mario ran laps.

109. Possessives and Adjectives

In a diagram a possessive noun, an article, or an adjective is placed on a slanted line under the noun it goes with.

SENTENCE **Carla's mother made a beautiful quilt.**

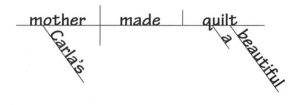

Diagram each of these sentences.

1. Sam's dad built a birdhouse.

2. I met Gina's cousin.

3. Tim's essay won first prize.

CONTINUED

Diagramming

4. We planted a large garden.

5. The young woman wore a yellow hat.

6. My new kitten has a long tail.

7. Megan read Chris's e-mail.

8. Paco's uncle bought a new car.

110. Adjective Complements

In a diagram an adjective used as a subject complement is placed on the horizontal line to the right of the verb. A slanted line that points back to the subject separates the verb and the subject complement.

SENTENCE **Harry's new shirt is blue.**

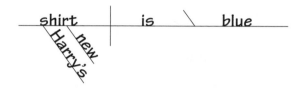

Diagram each of these sentences.

1. Carol's paintings are beautiful.

2. Gene is worried.

3. The movie was scary.

Diagramming

4. Tom's old bike is rusty.

5. The sheep's wool is soft.

6. Ethan's horse is intelligent.

7. The siren was loud.

8. Marta's little sister was excited.

111. Noun Complements

In a diagram a noun used as a subject complement is placed on the horizontal line to the right of the verb. A slanted line that points back toward the subject separates the verb and the subject complement.

SENTENCE **The tall man is my uncle.**

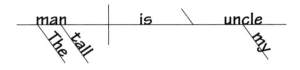

Diagram each of these sentences.

1. Soccer is Jason's favorite sport.

2. A trumpet is a wind instrument.

3. Chihuahuas are tiny dogs.

CONTINUED

Diagramming

4. Dana's best friend is Mark.

5. Math is Matt's best subject.

6. The cave was a perfect hideout.

7. Anna's dad is a good carpenter.

8. Cheetahs are speedy runners.

112. Adverbs

In a diagram an adverb goes on a slanted line under the verb that it tells about.

SENTENCE **Rick slurped the soup noisily.**

Diagram each of these sentences.

1. The horse galloped swiftly.

2. The little boy sobbed softly.

3. The bike's brakes squealed loudly.

4. My dad rarely cooks spaghetti.

5. The choir usually sings hymns.

6. Miranda quickly found the right page.

7. The birthday candles flickered brightly.

8. The frightened mouse scampered away.

113. Compounds—Part I

In a diagram of a sentence with a compound subject or a compound predicate, each subject and each predicate is placed on a separate horizontal line. The lines are parallel, and they are connected to the main horizontal line. The coordinating conjunction is written on a dashed line between the horizontal lines.

SENTENCE **Dogs and cats make good pets.**

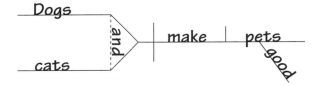

SENTENCE **The happy baby laughed and clapped.**

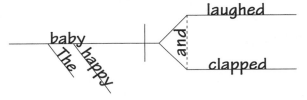

Diagram each of these sentences.

1. The orchestra and the chorus performed well.

2. Glenn and Maria washed the dishes.

CONTINUED

Diagramming

3. Caroline's sister sang and danced.

4. The old car rattled and coughed.

5. The team and the coaches celebrated the victory.

6. The playful kitten turned and ran.

7. Lucy and Alice carefully pulled the weeds.

114. Compounds—Part II

In a diagram a compound direct object is placed on two parallel horizontal lines connected to the main horizontal line. The coordinating conjunction is written on a dashed line between the two horizontal lines.

SENTENCE **The audience watched the clowns and the acrobats.**

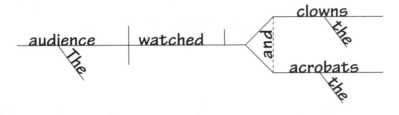

Diagram each of these sentences.

1. The hungry children ate sandwiches and fruit.

2. Paul's aunt fixed the toaster and the blender.

3. The boys wore mittens and parkas.

CONTINUED

Diagramming

4. The farmer raises cows and chickens.

5. My best friend plays the trumpet and the trombone.

6. The happy crowd waved flags and streamers.

7. Karen often cooks ham and eggs.

8. He rarely plays chess or checkers.

115. Compounds—Part III

In a diagram two or more nouns used as a compound subject complement are placed on parallel horizontal lines connected to the main horizontal line. The coordinating conjunction is written on a dashed line between the two horizontal lines.

SENTENCE **My dad is a scientist and an inventor.**

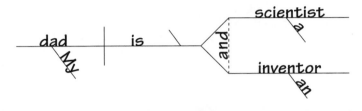

Diagram each of these sentences.

1. Ping's cousin is an actor and a magician.

2. My favorite shows are mysteries and comedies.

3. Our science project will be a model volcano or a barometer.

CONTINUED

Diagramming

4. His favorite presents were a watch and some binoculars.

5. Dinner tonight will be lasagna or meatloaf.

6. Kim's role will be an alien or an astronaut.

7. My uncles are farmers and ranchers.

8. The brick buildings are houses and stores.

116. Compounds—Part IV

In a diagram two or more adjectives used as a compound subject complement are placed on parallel horizontal lines connected to the main horizontal line. The coordinating conjunction is written on a dashed line between the two horizontal lines.

SENTENCE **The children were tired but happy.**

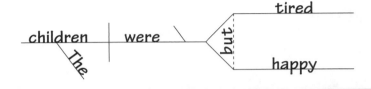

Diagram each of these sentences.

1. Our new teacher is funny and intelligent.

2. The lilies were tall and colorful.

3. The sailor's story was funny but mysterious.

4. The empty house was dark and scary.

5. The new trail was rocky and steep.

6. The fresh popcorn was hot and salty.

7. His old dog is slow and lazy.

8. Saturday will be sunny and mild.

Name _____

117. Compound Sentences

A compound sentence is diagrammed as two independent simple sentences. Each sentence is on its own horizontal line, one above the other. The coordinating conjunction is written on a dashed line that connects the two horizontal lines.

SENTENCE **I like tacos, but my sister prefers spaghetti.**

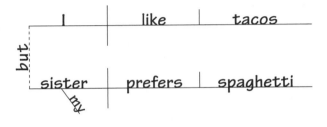

Diagram each of these sentences.

1. Dad washed his car, and Maya washed her bike.

2. The climb was difficult, but the view was spectacular.

3. Alice weeded the garden, and Keesha mowed the lawn.

4. This dinosaur was huge, and it ate meat.

5. The bird flew down, and it chirped loudly.

6. Cara likes fruit, but she rarely eats bananas.

7. The boy walked slowly, and he whistled a tune.

8. The team scored a goal, and everyone cheered.

118. Diagramming Practice

In a diagram, compound sentences or compound sentence parts go on separate horizontal lines. The coordinating conjunction goes on a dashed line that connects the horizontal lines.

Diagram each of these sentences.

1. My cousin ran fastest, and she won the race.

2. The babysitter and the children ate lunch outdoors.

3. The tiny black kitten mewed softly and licked my face.

4. Grandmother's flowers are tall and beautiful.

CONTINUED

Diagramming

5. The water was cold, but we waded across.

6. Rachel welcomed the guests and served the food.

7. The manager and the clerk filled the empty shelves.

8. The monster was scary, but he helped the little boy.

9. Henry bought a blue shirt and some tan pants.

Handbook of Terms

ADJECTIVES

An **adjective** is a word that points out or describes a noun.

Articles point out nouns. *A, an,* and *the* are articles: *A* pear and *an* apple are in *the* blue bowl.

Demonstrative adjectives point out specific persons, places, or things.

- *This* and *that* point out one person, place, or thing.
- *These* and *those* point out more than one person, place, or thing.
- *This* and *these* point out persons, places, or things that are near.
- *That* and *those* point out persons, places, or things that are farther away.

Descriptive adjectives give information about nouns.

- A descriptive adjective can come before a noun: *sunny* morning, *hot* day.
- A descriptive adjective that comes after a linking verb is a subject complement: The garden was *beautiful.*
- Some adjectives tell how many. They can tell exactly how many (*one, twelve, thirty*) or about how many (*several, few, many, some*).

Possessive adjectives show possession or ownership. A possessive adjective goes before a noun. The possessive adjectives are *my, your* (singular or plural), *his, her, its, our,* and *their: his* skateboard, *their* bikes.

Proper adjectives are adjectives that come from proper nouns. All other adjectives are called **common adjectives.** A proper adjective begins with a capital letter: *American* history.

See also **comparisons, sentences.**

ADVERBS

An **adverb** is a word that tells more about a verb.

- An **adverb of time** answers the question *when* or *how often:* It rained *yesterday.* We *usually* eat lunch at noon.
- An **adverb of place** answers the question *where:* Toshi bent his head *forward.* Sit *here* by the window.

137

- An **adverb of manner** answers the question *how:* She dances the waltz *gracefully.* Jason draws *well.*

A negative idea is expressed by using one negative word. That negative word may be *no, not, none, never,* or *nothing.* A sentence should contain only one negative word: I do not have *any* (not *no)* apples.

See also **comparisons.**

ANTECEDENTS

An **antecedent** is a word that a pronoun replaces. The pronoun must agree with its antecedent in person (first person, second person, or third person) and number (singular or plural). If the antecedent is third person singular, for example, the pronoun must be third person singular: *Kaye* ran because *she* was late. The pronouns *she, her,* and *hers* refer to females. The pronouns *he, him,* and *his* refer to males. The pronouns *it* and *its* refer to animals and things.

See also **pronouns.**

CAPITALIZATION

Many words begin with a capital letter, including the following:
- the first word of a sentence—The bell rang.
- an abbreviation if the word it stands for begins with a capital letter—U.S. government
- a title that goes before a person's name—Reverend Joseph Burke. When a title is abbreviated, it ends with a period—Sgt. Martha Wei.
- the first word and the name of the person addressed in the salutation of a letter and the first word in the closing of a letter—Dear Marie, Yours truly,
- the first word, the last word, and each important word in the titles of books, plays, works of art, and poems—*A Tale of Two Cities, Romeo and Juliet, Starry Night,* "Fire and Ice"
- the first word of a direct quotation—Dad said, "Let's visit the aquarium."
- proper nouns such as the names of people, pets, streets, cities, states, countries, days, months, holidays—Abraham Lincoln, Pine Street, United States of America
- proper adjectives—American flag, Dutch cocoa

Capital letters are also used for:

- the pronoun *I*
- two-letter state postal abbreviations—MA, NY, CA
- an initial (a capital letter followed by a period). A person may use initials or an initial instead of a name—J. K. Rowling.

COMPARISONS

Many adjectives can be used to compare two or more persons, places, or things.

- To compare two persons, places, or things, *-er* may be added to most adjectives: *taller, cuter, hungrier, bigger.*
- To compare three or more persons, places, or things, *-est* may be added to the adjective: *meanest, nicest, happiest, hottest.*
- Some adjectives that compare use *more* and *most* instead of *-er* or *-est.* Adjectives with three or more syllables usually use *more* or *most. More* is used to compare two persons, places, or things. *Most* is used to compare three or more persons, places, or things: *more delicious, most delicious.*
- Some adjectives that compare are **irregular adjectives.** They are not formed by adding *-er* or *-est: good, better, best* and *bad, worse, worst.*

Fewer and *fewest* are used with plural count nouns: There are *fewer* apples than oranges. *Less* and *least* are used with noncount nouns: My car uses *less* gas than yours.

Adverbs can be used to compare two or more actions.

- To compare two actions, add *-er* to the adverb or put *more* before the adverb: *faster, more carefully.*
- To compare three or more actions, add *-est* to the adverb or put *most* before the adverb: *fastest, most carefully.*

CONJUNCTIONS

A **conjunction** is a word used to connect words or groups of words.

A **coordinating conjunction** connects words or groups of words that are similar. The most common coordinating conjunctions are *and, but,* and *or:* Joshua *or* Leanne will cut out the words. Nancy drew *and* colored the pictures. Mika glued the words on the poster, *but* Carla glued the pictures.

CONTRACTIONS

A **contraction** is two words written as one word with one or more letters missing. An apostrophe (') is used to show a missing letter or letters. Subject pronouns are used with some verbs to form contractions: *we're* for *we are, she's* for *she is.*

NOUNS

A **noun** is a word that names a person, place, or thing. A noun can be used as the subject, the direct object, or the subject complement in a sentence.

A noun that names a group of persons or things is called a **collective noun**: The *band* played loudly.

A **common noun** names any one member of a group of persons, places, or things: *queen, city, church.*

Count nouns name items that can be counted separately. A count noun has a singular and a plural form: *cherries, emotions, chairs.*

A noun is used in **direct address** when it names the person spoken to: *Hannah,* would you help me?

Noncount nouns name items that cannot be counted separately. A noncount noun has only a singular form: *fruit, anger, furniture.*

A **plural noun** names more than one person, place, or thing.

- To form the plural of most nouns, add *-s* or *-es* to the singular noun: *boys, ranches, berries.*
- The plural of an **irregular noun** is not formed by adding *-s* or *-es*: *men, children, wolves, teeth, fish.*

A **proper noun** names a particular person, place, or thing. A proper noun begins with a capital letter: *Queen Elizabeth, London, Westminster Abbey.*

A **possessive noun** expresses possession or ownership. The apostrophe (') is the sign of a possessive noun.

- To form the possessive of a singular noun, add *-'s* to the singular form: *architect's*
- To form the possessive of a plural noun that ends in *-s*, add an apostrophe to the plural form: *farmers'*
- To form the possessive of a plural noun that does not end in *-s*, add *-'s* to the plural form: *children's*

A **singular noun** names one person, place, or thing: *boy, ranch, berry.*

See also **sentences.**

PRONOUNS

A **pronoun** is a word that takes the place of a noun or nouns.

A **personal pronoun** has different forms. A personal pronoun shows **person** (first person, second person, or third person) and **number** (singular or plural).

- A **first person** pronoun refers to the person speaking. The pronouns that refer to the speaker are *I, me, mine, we, us,* and *ours.*

- A **second person** pronoun refers to the person or people spoken to. The pronouns that refer to the person or people spoken to are *you* and *yours. You* and *yours* can be either singular or plural: Where did *you* go, *Carrie?* Where did *you* go, *girls?*

- A **third person** pronoun refers to the person, place, or thing spoken about. The third person pronouns are *he, him, his, she, her, hers, it, its, they, them,* and *theirs.*

- A **singular** pronoun refers to one person, place, or thing. The singular pronouns are *I, me, mine, you, yours, she, her, hers, he, him, his, it,* and *its.*

- A **plural** pronoun refers to more than one person, place or thing. The plural pronouns are *we, us, ours, you, yours, they, them,* and *theirs.*

Subject pronouns may be used as the subject of a sentence. The subject pronouns are *I, you* (singular or plural), *he, she, it, we,* and *they: He* bought a new car.

- A compound subject may contain one or more subject pronouns. They are connected by *and* or *or: He* and Margie are in the park. Joe and *she* are playing tennis. *He* or *she* will win the game.

An **object pronoun** may be used as the direct object of a sentence. The object pronouns are *me, you* (singular or plural), *him, her, it, us,* and *them:* I saw *her* at the mall.

A **possessive pronoun** shows possession or ownership. The possessive pronouns are *mine, yours, his, hers, its, ours,* and *theirs.* They are not placed before nouns. Although possessive pronouns show ownership, they do not contain apostrophes: The new skates are *hers.*

See also **antecedents, sentences, subject-verb agreement.**

PUNCTUATION

Punctuation is used to make writing clearer.

An **apostrophe** (') is used as follows:

- to show ownership—the *cook's* hat, the *girls'* horses, the *children's* toys
- to replace letters left out in a contraction—*he'll* for *he will, I'm* for *I am*

A **comma** (,) can be used in many ways, including the following:

- to separate three or more words or groups of words in a series—We saw elephants, giraffes, hyenas, and monkeys.
- to set off parts of dates—January 1, 2009
- to set off parts of addresses—321 Spring Rd., Apt. 4
- to separate a city and a state—Atlanta, GA
- to set off words in direct address—Josie, I'm so pleased that you called me this morning.
- after the word *yes* or *no* when it introduces a sentence—Yes, I agree with you completely.
- to set off a direct quotation, unless a question mark or an exclamation point is needed—
    "We have only vanilla and chocolate today," he said
  in a sad voice.
    "Great!" shouted Lena.
- to separate simple sentences connected by the conjunctions *and, but,* or *or*—She called his name, but he didn't answer her.
- after the salutation in a friendly letter and the closing in all letters—Dear Ben, Sincerely yours,

An **exclamation point** (!) is used at the end of an exclamatory sentence: What a celebration that was!

A **period** (.) is used at the end of a declarative sentence or an imperative sentence and after initials and some abbreviations: Dr. H. L. Martin is here. Please invite him to sit down.

A **question mark** (?) is used at the end of a question: What time is it?

Quotation marks (" ") are used as follows:

- before and after every direct quotation and every part of a divided quotation—
    "Let's go shopping," said Michiko.
    "I can go with you," Father said, "after I have eaten lunch."

- to enclose titles of short stories, poems, and magazine articles. Titles of books, magazines, newspapers, movies, TV shows and works of art are usually printed in *italics* or are underlined—I read "A Tribute to Heroes" in *Time for Kids.*

SENTENCES

A **sentence** is a group of words that expresses a complete thought. A sentence has a subject and a predicate.

The **subject** names the person, place, or thing a sentence is about.

- The **simple subject** is a noun or pronoun: The *man* is riding his bike.
- The **complete subject** is the simple subject and all the words that go with it: *The tall young man* is riding his bike.
- A subject pronoun may be used as the subject of a sentence: *We* went to the mall.
- If a sentence has more than one simple subject, it has a **compound subject:** *Ivan* and *John* argued with the grocer.

The **predicate** tells what the subject is or does.

- The **simple predicate** is a verb or verb phrase: Teresa *waved.*
- The **complete predicate** is the verb and all the words relating to it: Teresa *waved from the window.*
- If a sentence has more than one simple predicate, it has a **compound predicate:** Our hamster *eats* and *exercises* at night.

A **direct object** is a noun or a pronoun that receives the action of a verb. A direct object answers the question *whom* or *what* after an action verb in a sentence: Nathaniel fed the *baby.*

- An object pronoun can be used as a direct object: Nathaniel fed *him.*
- If a sentence has more than one direct object, it has a **compound direct object:** Wear your *hat, scarf,* and *gloves.*

A **subject complement** is a word that completes the meaning of a linking verb in a sentence. A subject complement is usually a noun or an adjective: Broccoli is a green *vegetable.* The sea will be *cold.*

- If a sentence has more than one subject complement, it has a **compound subject complement:** The winners were *Steve* and *Patty.*

A **compound sentence** contains two short sentences that are related to each other. They are combined with a comma, followed by *and, but,* or *or.* We went to the park, *and* we played softball. It started to rain, *but* we kept playing.

A **declarative sentence** makes a statement. It ends with a period: The sun is shining.

An **exclamatory sentence** expresses strong or sudden emotion. It ends with an exclamation point: What a loud noise that was!

An **imperative sentence** gives a command or makes a request. It usually ends with a period: Go to the store. Please pick up the papers.

An **interrogative sentence** asks a question. It ends with a question mark: Where is my pen?

A **run-on sentence** results when two sentences are combined but are not connected correctly. To combine two sentences correctly, put a comma and *and, but,* or *or* after the first sentence: We will play checkers, *or* we will watch a movie.

SUBJECT-VERB AGREEMENT

A subject and its verb must agree.

- In the simple present tense, singular nouns and the pronouns *he, she,* and *it* take verbs that end in *-s* or *-es:* The boy *runs.* He *runs.*

- In the simple present tense, plural nouns, plural subject pronouns (*we, you,* and *they*), and the subject pronouns *I* and *you* take verbs that do not end in *-s* or *-es:* Dogs *run.* We *run.* You *run.* They *run.* I *run.*

- Use *am* or *was* with the pronoun *I:* I *am* a soccer player. I *was* late for practice.

- Use *is* or *was* with a singular noun or a third person singular subject pronoun (*he, she,* and *it*): Paris *is* a city. She *was* a pianist.

- Use *are* or *were* with a plural noun, the second person subject pronoun (*you*), the first person plural pronoun (*we*), or the third person plural pronoun (*they*): Dogs *are* good pets. You *are* the winner. We *were* happy. They *were* my neighbors.

- Use *does* with a singular noun or a singular third person subject pronoun (*he, she,* and *it*): Harry *does* his homework after school. She *does* research on the computer.

- Use *do* with a plural noun, the first person subject pronoun (*I* and *we*), a second person subject pronoun (*you*), or the third person plural subject pronoun (*they*): The children *do* the dishes every night. You *do* your work well. They *do* their best.

- When a sentence starts with *there is, there are, there was,* or *there were,* the subject follows the verb. The verb must agree with the subject: There *is* a *dog* on the porch. There *were* three *mistakes* on my paper.

TENSE

The tense of a verb shows when its action happens.

- The **simple present tense** tells about an action that is always true or that happens again and again: I *play* the piano every afternoon.

- The **simple past tense** tells about an action that happened in the past. The simple past of a regular verb is formed by adding *-d* or *-ed*: I *played* the piano yesterday afternoon. The simple past of an irregular verb is not formed by adding *-d* or *-ed*: I *sang.* They *wrote.* She *came.*

- The **future tense** tells about an action that will happen in the future. The future tense can be formed in two ways. It can be formed with the helping verb *will* and the present: Matt and Kiya *will see* a concert. The future tense can also be made with a form of the verb *be* (*am, are, is*), followed by the phrase *going to* and the present form of the main verb: We *are going to play* softball. I *am going to visit* the museum.

- The **present progressive tense** tells what is happening now. The present progressive tense is formed with a present form of *be* and the present participle: He *is washing* his hands now.

- The **past progressive tense** tells what was happening in the past. The past progressive tense is formed with a past form of *be* and the present participle: He *was skipping* when I saw him.

- The **present perfect tense** tells about an action that happened at some indefinite time in the past or an action that started in the past and continues into the present time. The present perfect tense is formed with *has* or *have* and the past participle: I *have read* that book. We *have lived* here for two years.

- The **past perfect tense** tells about a past action that was completed before another action in the past. The past perfect tense is formed with *had* and the past participle: She *had finished* her homework by 6 o'clock. Mike *had watched* the fish before he went to sleep.

- The **future perfect tense** tells about a future event that will be completed before another future event. The future perfect tense is formed with *will have* and the past participle: We *will have eaten* lunch by the time you get here.

VERBS

An **action verb** is a word that tells what someone or something does: Jake *sings.* The dog *barked.*

A **being verb** shows what someone or something is. Being verbs do not express action. A being verb is often a **linking verb.** A linking verb joins the subject of a sentence to a subject complement (a noun or an adjective): They *are* firemen. He *is* happy.

A **helping verb** is always followed by a main verb. Some helping verbs are *am, is, are, was, were, be, being, been, shall, will, may, can, has, have, had, do, does, did, should, would, could,* and *must:* Mom *is washing* the dishes. I *will help* her.

A verb has four **principal parts: the present,** the **present participle,** the **past,** and the **past participle.**

- The present participle is formed by adding *-ing* to the present: *jumping, writing, hopping.* For verbs that end in *e,* drop the final *e* and add *-ing:* write, writing. For verbs that end in a consonant following a vowel, double the consonant before adding *-ing:* hop, hopping. The present participle is used with a form of the helping verb *be:* I *am jumping.* She *was writing.* They *are hopping.*

- The simple past and the past participle of **regular verbs** are formed by adding *-d or -ed* to the present: *saved, jumped.* For verbs that end in a consonant following a vowel, form the past participle by doubling the consonant before adding *-ed: hum, hummed.* The past participle is used with a helping verb such as *has, have,* or *had:* I *have jumped.* She *has written.* They *had hopped.*

- The simple past and the past participle of **irregular verbs** are not formed by adding *-d or -ed* to the present: *sing, sang, sung.*

A **verb phrase** is made up of one or more helping verbs (such as *is, are, has, have, will, can, could, would, should*) and a main verb: She *must wear* her hat.